For the Believers

A Guidebook to Manifesting Abundance,
Increasing Your Financial Net Worth,
Restoring the Papercuts in Your Soul, and
Transforming Your Life!

Loretta (La-Rue') Duncan-Fowler

Table of Contents

Introduction

When you focus on becoming a blessing, God makes sure that you are always blessed in abundance. —Joel Osteen

Welcome to transforming your life and achieving your goals the Biblical way by aligning your mindset with abundance principles and taking intentional steps so that you will succeed! If you're seeking to create a life of abundance and prosperity, it's essential to understand that your thoughts, beliefs, and actions play a significant role in shaping your reality. Manifesting abundance requires courage, commitment, and a positive attitude, which can transform your life in ways you never thought possible.

You may feel depressed and exhausted. You may feel like you've done everything you could to achieve your goals, but you still don't see the light. Maybe you've experienced traumatic events that trampled on your self-worth and confidence, and now the struggle is manifesting into your physical reality through your finances, relationships, and health. Regardless of your situation and how you're feeling right now, please keep Jesus's words in mind: "I am the light of the world. Whoever follows me will not walk in darkness, but will have the light of life" (*NIV,* 2011/1973, John 8:12).

This is God's promise for your life. You will not walk in darkness, but instead, inherit the light of life.

I'm sure you are wondering what having a paper cut has to do with living an abundant life. Please humor me for a moment.

As I was taking stock of my life, which is something I tend to do around the new year, the Holy Spirit impressed upon me that even though I had done a lot of work to heal spiritually, physically, and financially, I still had small paper cuts in my soul that could only be healed by Him. I knew this was true because I was still struggling in certain areas; the small, miniscule areas that all the prayers in the world didn't seem to help and I felt that struggle would go on forever. But the Bible says in Hebrews: "That God will make you perfect in every good work to do his will, working in you that which is well pleasing in his sight, through Jesus Christ; to whom be glory forever and ever. Amen" (*KJV*, 2021/1611, Hebrews 13:21).

God will make me perfect in every good work that is pleasing to Him. My paper cuts will heal, and I will be restored and so will you!

According to Wiktionary, the definition of a paper cut is this: a wound caused by a piece of paper or a thin, sharp material which can slice through a person's skin (2023).

Paper cuts are extremely small and painful. They take longer to heal because they are tiny but sometimes feel the most painful. They don't bleed as much. In fact, it takes longer for the chemicals in your blood to heal your paper cut than to heal your body. Imagine that! (Bonaguro, 2015)

The same is true for healing the broken pieces in your soul. There are small paper cuts that need to be healed, and when that happens, you can achieve a fulfilling, abundant, and prosperous life.

In my experience, that healing can only take place with the help and love of the Holy Spirit. The glory of the kingdom of God offers complete healing and restoration in your body, mind, and spirit. The Bible states in Matthew, "Howbeit this kind goeth not out but by prayer and fasting" (*KJV*, 2021/1611, Matthew 17:21).

Surely, prayer works. Fasting also works when you're seeking clarity. You may have read every self-help book known to man (or woman), attended workshops on self-improvement, went to spiritual conferences, received therapy, and visited your spiritual app multiple times a day to gain comfort in the daily devotion it offers you. I know those things are helpful. I have done the same and have made great strides in my healing journey. But prayer is the surefire thing that can help give you all that you need.

This book will take you on a journey of healing and self-discovery so that you can finally achieve the full abundant life that you've been yearning for.

But, let me tell you this: This book is not for everyone. It is not for the faint of heart. To heal can be very challenging. It takes time, patience, and a deep, spiritual encounter with the Lord to fully heal. This book is not for the Unbelievers, although if you read it, I pray that you come to know Christ as your Savior and you become a Believer.

This book is for those who:

- Believe that walking a spiritual path with Christ is the key to healing and abundance, and they want to find out how they can begin walking that path.

- Are ready to seek change and transformation and increase their faith and trust in God as they move toward an abundant life.

- Are ready to experience healing from past trauma.

- Are ready to move forward into a life of faith, abundance, and growth.

- Want to live happy and healthy, knowing and understanding that the only way to achieve this is to seek a relationship with God our Savior.

In Hebrew 11, it says: "And without faith, it is impossible to please God, because anyone who comes to him must believe that he exists and that he rewards those who earnestly seek him" (*NIV*, 2011/1973, Hebrews 11:6).

The prerequisite for this book is that you first believe that there is a God, that you are His Creation, and that He loves you. To accomplish this, the only step you need to take can be found in Romans:

"That if you confess with your mouth, 'Jesus is Lord,' and believe in your heart that God raised him from the dead, you will be saved. For it is with your heart that you believe and are justified, and it is with your mouth that you profess your faith and are saved" (*NIV*, 2011/1973, Romans 10:9-10).

Secondly, believe that He is a rewarder of those who diligently seek Him.

I can testify to this because the more I sought God and His will for my life, the more blessed and greater my life became. He is a keeper of promises, a way maker when it doesn't feel like there is a way. If you continue to seek Him, He will reward you and provide astounding abundance for your life. In Matthew 6:33, it says, "To seek ye first the kingdom of God and His righteousness and all these things shall be added unto you" (*KJV*, 1987/1611).

In other words, we put God first when we worship Him, praise Him, thank Him, trust Him, and rely on Him rather than ourselves or anyone else. We seek God first when we go to Him for comfort, strength, and reassurance as we acknowledge who He is and what He can do. Thirdly, with the faith of a mustard seed, you can achieve anything you desire.

For context, it is here in Matthew: "Truly I tell you, if you have faith as small as a mustard seed, you can say to this mountain, 'Move from here to there,' and it will move." Nothing will be impossible for you" (*NIV*, 2011/1973, Matthew 17:20).

Nothing is ever impossible for God. He seeks to provide healing and restoration for your life, even if it feels like there is no way out. This book offers you the light of God's righteousness. Using God's word, it is here to help you heal. It is here to help restore you from any iniquities you may be experiencing so your faith can increase, and you may witness God's love and protection in your life.

It is my hope that you can experience freedom and peace through a rebirth into the kingdom of God, where abundance, peace, healing, and restoration are the norm in your finances, relationships, mental health, spiritual health, and career or business. This is my solemn vow to you.

Are you ready to achieve the abundant life you've been seeking? Let's heal that paper cut!

Chapter 1:

Looking Through Corrective Lenses: Seeing Yourself the Way God Sees You

I remember the first time I needed glasses. When I was a young girl, I was always walking into things. When I was in school, I would sit in the front row to see the board. During class, I thought the way that I saw the board was the way everyone saw it. My teacher could not understand why I was failing because I was an exceptionally smart child. At the time, I didn't realize that my perception of what I was looking at on the board was incorrect.

When I walked into something or tripped over something, I assumed that I was just a clumsy, uncoordinated kid. I remember playing with my cousins. We were running through my aunt's three-story Victorian home, and I ran right into the door frame. I missed the door opening by a mile–to this day, I still have the gash on my forehead.

My cousins laughed while I cried. At the time, it wasn't funny–it hurt a lot! But now, looking back, it was funny because the door was wide open. After many hysterics, my aunt told my grandparents what happened, and they ended up telling my parents that I needed glasses.

My parents believed that I was just an uncoordinated, accident-prone, clumsy kid until my grades started going downhill, and the school nurse decided to test my vision. She realized that I needed glasses, so my parents took me to the eye doctor, and guess what happened? The doctor said that it was a miracle that I had made it through life thus far because I was severely nearsighted. Imagine that!

Once I received my new glasses, everything changed. The entire world as I knew it was clearer, brighter, and more beautiful. Everything was colorful—the trees were greener, the sky was bluer, and I could run and play without hurting myself. Most importantly, my grades improved tremendously. I could finally see and understand what the teacher was teaching, instead of my perception being altered to what I thought was being taught.

This chapter is about shifting your perspective. Just like in my story, at times we may have difficulty seeing things clearly. We may have a different perception; a more logical and rational perception than what is truly meant to be for our lives. This chapter will address why it's important to start looking at yourself the way God sees you. It's a brighter perspective. It might not even make sense right now, but His perception is always greater.

We'll be discussing a few key points:

- The importance of changing how you see yourself.

- The importance of understanding how God sees you.

- The importance of shifting your thought patterns and correcting them so you can begin to see yourself through God's eyes, instead of your own.

At the end of the chapter, I will share a few bible verses with you to meditate on as you move on to Chapter Two.

Changing How You See Yourself

The first step in improving your life is changing your perception of yourself and seeing yourself the way God sees you.

The Bible states in John: "The thief comes only to steal and kill and destroy; I have come that they may have life and have it to the full" (*NIV*, 2011/1973, John 10:10). The lie that my parents told me unintentionally was that I was clumsy, uncoordinated, and accident-prone. The truth was that I needed glasses.

However, even with new glasses, I still experienced low self-esteem in both my mind and spirit. I was clumsy, uncoordinated, and accident prone, and now the kids bullied me for having four eyes instead of two.

It is important you learn to see yourself through the spiritual lenses that God sees you, not through your physical, corrective lenses. If you begin to see yourself through God's eyes, the bullying and the limiting beliefs people made up about you will seem inconsequential.

Isaiah 43:4, says: "Since you are precious and honored in my sight, and because I love you, I will give people in exchange for you, nations in exchange for your life" (*NIV*, 2011/1973).

God sees us as precious and worthy of respect. Our perception of how we view ourselves is important if we want to transform our lives and achieve the life we desire.

When you believe the lie that has been sowed into your spirit by the enemy (Satan), the perception of yourself is distorted. It is important to believe in the truth—that is, how God sees you; perfect and wonderfully made. "For you created my inmost being; you knit me together in my mother's womb. I praise you because I am fearfully and wonderfully made; your works are wonderful, I know that full well" (*NIV*, 2011/1973, Psalm 139:13, 14). The first step in obtaining an abundant life is to see yourself how God sees you. If you allow your perception to shift to how God sees you, your life will begin to change.

So often, as we go through the motions merely to survive, or as we race toward the finish line, we get stuck with listening to the enemy's voice in our head. And then we lose sight of our goals and our dreams. Every time we attempt to succeed at something, the enemy tries to sow lies into our spirit, causing us to lose sight of God's remarkable plans for our life. We get so caught up with shame and deceit—it's as if we've lost our identity, our sense of who we are through Jesus Christ. But if we allow ourselves to come back into our spirit, to come back home to God's love and tenderness, knowing and believing that He has already won our battles against the enemy, we can trust full well that our life will be righteous, and we will experience God's full abundance.

God Sees You Differently

For the Lord seeth not as man seeth; for man looketh on the outward appearance, but the Lord looketh on the heart. –I Samuel 16:7

I want you to know something–something that should be so apparent, but most people neglect: God sees, recognizes, and embraces you at a far greater level than you may ever know. He doesn't care about how coiffed your hair is, whether your nails are perfectly shaped and manicured, or how much money you have in your bank account. Whether you have $1 or $10,000, God sees you for who you truly are.

You are a child of God, there is no doubt about that. "See what great love the Father has lavished on us, that we should be called children of God! And that is what we are! The reason the world does not know us is that it did not know him" (*NIV*, 2011/1973, 1 John 3:1). At times, this truth may recede to the back of our mind, and we begin to focus on how others see us. We focus on the clothes that we wear, the car we drive, the house we live in, and whether we are raising our children at the best schools. We compare ourselves to others and try to compete, so we don't get left behind and forgotten. We try to be the best, so people notice us. But God sees us, His children, differently. Even if people don't notice us, God notices us. He sees our heart and soul, rather than our outward appearance just as 1 Samuel 16:7 explains. It's what is in your heart that matters, not what you look like and what you have. You can be a poor, homeless pauper, and God will still see you as His perfect child. He knows what's in your heart, and He will always provide and not forget for you.

There are many people in this world that will judge us and perhaps even try to condemn us based on what we look like, what we have, what we don't have, or a combination of all three. But God is different. He is the God of righteousness. The God that is more than enough and will give us everything we need and want if we ask for it in prayer. He is an all-mighty, all-powerful loving God, but also a fair God. He treats every single one of us equally and with the same love and compassion regardless of what we have and don't have.

We must recognize how God sees us so we can live our life, knowing that we are unconditionally loved and supported by God's grace and constant abundance. We must acknowledge that God sees us differently than the way man sees us. His perception of His children is noble. Absolute. Never changing. Righteous. He sees our hearts. And He loves us because of it.

Adjusting Your Thought Patterns

Therefore, with minds that are alert and fully sober, set your hope on the grace to be brought to you when Jesus Christ is revealed at his coming. –1 Peter 1:13

There are three important thought patterns we need to correct and shift to live an abundant life with God as our Savior. Without correcting them, these thought patterns live on in our spirit and limit us as we navigate life's challenges. These patterns have the potential to destroy our very being and allow the enemy to attack us at our core.

Just as it says in 1 Peter 1:14, we are obedient children. We need to ensure our minds are fully alert and sober so we can take the actions we need to take to rectify our limitations. As we begin the journey of correction, it is important that we not only believe in ourselves but believe in the Holy Spirit that God will work through us and bring healing and restoration to our minds and spirit.

I Need to Feel Loved and Accepted by Everyone

As humans, we seek constant love and affection. We crave to be loved and accepted by every person we meet. Since we were kids, we toyed with the notion of acceptance. We sought approval from the popular kids; if the popular kids thought we were cool, then so would everyone else. If not, we'd experience bullying and torment.

At times, we craved acceptance so badly that we would do other people's homework and buy things for them as a bribe so they could celebrate us and call us their friends. If we finally had the opportunity to get into the popular kid's good graces, they would tell us what to wear and how to act.

"If you want to become popular, you need to change your clothes."

"You can't have your hair like that. It looks stupid."

"No one in their right mind would wear those shoes."

We took in all the torment and humiliation just so we could be liked and approved of by the most popular kids in school. Little did we know they were taking our power away and crushing our self-worth inch by inch. They started to rule our identity and dictate who we need to be. And because we wore the veil of acceptance every single day, we never realized that is what they were doing.

As we grew into adulthood, seeking external validation progressed into more extravagant things. The type of car you drive, what your house looks like, whether or not you're married, the amount of money you make, the type of job you have—all these things contribute to your thought pattern of, "I will do anything I can to be liked and accepted by everyone." Again, the veil of acceptance became our disguise to be approved and liked by our neighbors, coworkers, and friends.

To correct this, here's what I want you to know: Your identity stands, and will always stand, in Jesus Christ. He approves of you, regardless of what you look like or what you have. Remember 1 Samuel 16:7? God doesn't look at your outward appearance, but rather, he looks at your heart. As a child and later as an adult, you may have lost your identity and given its power to the bullies and to those whom you were seeking validation from, but I encourage you to remember that your identity and your character are always rooted in the Lord, our Savior. He stands by you, no matter what. He loves, supports, and guides you unconditionally, and there is nothing that you ask in His name that He won't give you (Matthew 7:7-8). It's okay to take off the veil because you don't need to seek acceptance from your Father. You have already been accepted by Jesus since before you were born. Your self-worth is never determined by man but by your identity in Jesus Christ. I encourage you to ask yourself, "Who am I?"–not in the context of, "Who am I to my spouse/coworkers/partners/friends?" Instead, ask yourself, "Who am I in Jesus Christ?"

My Past Experiences Determine Who I Am and How I Act Right Now

There are many things in our past that we wish we could take back. Things that we feel guilty about or feel like we are being condemned for. Things that made us feel like we needed to hide our true selves from others in fear of judgment, criticism, or persecution. Things that created a mess in our lives and now we are in the middle of cleaning it up and picking up the pieces.

All these things from our past shaped our identity and character. They created a persona that perhaps we're not proud of, so we walk around feeling ashamed of who we have become. They now influence every decision we make in our lives, and because of what happened in our past, we feel bound and chained to a life full of regret, shame, deceit, and embarrassment.

There is something I want you to know. This is the enemy talking. The devil wants us to continue feeling shame, guilt, and resentment. He wants us to feel that we are bound to our past mistakes so he can continue to win our souls. It is important, for the betterment of our lives, that we have the courage to overcome our past issues and fully heal from them so that we can rejoice with our Lord Jesus Christ. God never wants us to suffer. He never wants us to feel pain or regret or feel like we are being controlled by what we experienced in the past. He wants us to rejoice in Him.

Be still and know that I am God. –Psalm 46:10

God wants us to treasure life with Him and move forward in peace and harmony. He wants us to realize that all our struggles and our battles have been won by Him. We must confess our sins to God so that we may be restored and healed all the days of our life. "If we confess our sins, God is faithful and just to forgive us our sins and cleanse us from all unrighteousness" (*KJV*, 1987/1611, 1 John 1:9). By confessing our sins to our Lord Jesus Christ, He heals our mind and spirit and restores us from any wrongdoings from our past and otherwise.

Know that your past no longer defines you. What defines you is who you are in Christ Jesus (Psalms 82:6). Whatever you have done in your past, you are forgiven. Christ forgives you. He died on the cross and sacrificed His life for you, so you don't have to live under the yoke of sin and condemnation: "There is therefore now no condemnation to them which are in Christ Jesus, who walk not after the flesh, but after the Spirit" (*KJV*, 1987/1611, Romans 8:1).

This is love: not that we loved God, but that he loved us and sent his Son as an atoning sacrifice for our sins. —1 John 4:10

Why Don't I Feel Worthy, Competent, Intelligent, and Successful Enough?

You strive for perfection in every area of your life. There is no room for error, and if there was, you beat yourself up and constantly affirm to yourself that you're not enough or worthy of receiving abundance.

You compare yourself to others, and the only momentum you have in your life is that of judgment, criticism, and feeling unworthy and unsuccessful. So many people struggle with anxiety and depression because they feel like they cannot live up to the perfect standards of society, have high expectations of themselves, and don't feel they can live up to their own standards.

You've created a meaning of perfection in your mind, but to you, that does not include the credentials you offer or the amount of success you've achieved, nor does it include having unconditional love and respect for yourself and others. This innate idea of perfection includes striving for success that feels difficult for you to achieve, but you practically exhaust all your energy trying to achieve any amount that remotely comes close to it.

Two words come to mind when I think about correcting this pattern: God's Grace. God has given you His grace to mess up and find your own identity. Sometimes, your journey may divert away from God's love, but that doesn't mean He has left you stranded. He's around to protect you from false teachings and to remind you that you are always enough in His eyes. When we feel unworthy of our own success, it is important to remember to come humbly before God and seek His wisdom, salvation, and healing. Ask for His grace to be poured unto you so your spirit may be bountifully restored.

Meditation

Now that we've gone through and corrected our thought patterns, which has given us some encouragement, I encourage you to meditate on the following verses. You can journal about them if you wish. The main purpose is to try to reflect on how these verses speak to you so you can understand what they mean for you and your life.

- Jeremiah 1:5

- Matthew 10:28-31

- 1 Peter 5:7

In this chapter, we spoke about so many things that can successfully set you up for abundance as you move forward with your life. By now, we know how important it is to see yourself in the way that God sees you. We understand what we need to do to change our perception of how we view ourselves, and we also learned why it's important to correct our thought patterns as we move forward, striving for a harmonious life in God's kingdom.

The next chapter will reveal so many great things about abundance and what it means in the biblical sense. We'll be discussing the importance of why we need to strive for abundance in every area of our lives; and no, I'm not only talking about financial abundance. I'm referring to heavenly abundance with God as our Savior, healer, and restorer of all things. It is important that when we seek abundance, we ask God to give it to us in the fruit of the spirit, rather than strive for man-made abundance. Chapter Two will discuss how we can do this successfully so we can achieve God's abundance in every area of our lives. We are no longer surviving, but we are striving—this next chapter will show you how.

Chapter 2:

Choosing the Abundant Life

When I think of abundance, I think of this: There is no magic potion.

I've always believed that the decisions you make in life determine the outcome and how your life plays out. It is safe to say that in the current world, we live in, some things are out of our control. For example, you cannot pick your parents when you are born (they are given to you by God), and you cannot choose to be born into a rich family or a poor one. Situations such as these simply happen. They are beyond our human control. In Psalms 66:22, this is exactly what Psalmist King David was saying.

However, regardless of how you grew up or what your current circumstances are, you can choose abundance. You can choose to live in abundance, or you can choose to live in scarcity. Many people believe they are dealt with the scarcity card; it's as if they feel they've been punished, but the fact of the matter is that they are experiencing scarcity because of the decisions they've made.

Here's an example of what I mean in my own life:

Many people do not know this about me, but I grew up on Aid to Families with Dependent Children (AFDC) in Massachusetts. Another term for this would be called welfare.

AFDC was established by the Social Security Act of 1935 (U.S. Department of Health & Human Services) as a grant program to allow states to provide cash welfare payments for needy children who have been deprived of parental support or care because their father or mother was absent from the home, incapacitated, deceased, or unemployed.

My parents divorced when I was approximately five years old. We relied on public assistance 95 percent of the time until I was approximately 18 years old.

Now, the last time I checked; my net worth is 1.5 million dollars.

So, my question for you is this: How does a little girl born in the sixties to divorced parents and on AFDC for over 13 years go from living in poverty for all her childhood to becoming a multi-millionaire?

This is how—I believed. And I decided.

I believed everything that the Word of God said about me. I looked up as many biblical scriptures as I could find on abundance and prosperity. I was determined to change my story and my life. I refused to believe that poverty was all God had intended for me. I refused to believe that I would be broke, busted, and disgusted for the rest of my life. I chose to change my history, so my children didn't have to go through what I experienced during much of my childhood.

I also felt a lot of gratitude for the circumstances I was living in and being born into. My parents may not have had a lot of money, but I had a roof over my head, food in my stomach, and clothes on my back, and I was blessed to be able to read and write. My mother said I even learned to tie my shoes by the time I was two years old; this prompted her to enroll me in kindergarten at an early age.

As I said in the beginning, there is no magic potion for abundance. When you decide that you are abundant in every way, you will begin to truly live it. I never felt poor, and this was probably because of the neighborhood that I grew up in. Many of my friends and schoolmates were in similar situations. I was blatantly aware of the stigma that we received when we used food stamps to eat, received government cheese and powdered milk, or even government rations such as canned meat. But even though we encountered stigma and judgment because of the situation we found ourselves in for years, I quickly learned that other people's perceptions were not my problem—it was theirs and has been all along. I learned that it was a waste of my good energy to change the perceptions of ignorant people.

Psalm 23:1 says, "The Lord is my shepherd, I lack nothing" (*NIV*, 2011/1973). God always blesses us with abundance every single day of our lives. When we can truly understand this, scarcity will no longer be a part of our day-to-day life, and we will learn to choose better. This chapter is about helping us decipher what it means to be truly abundant in God's eyes. Through the eyes of the Spirit, we can experience ultimate abundance, glory, and righteousness.

This chapter will explain the following:

- What it means to live an abundant life.

- Ways to attract an abundant mindset.

- The importance of choosing differently.

- How to decode the true meaning of abundance (Hint: there's more to abundance than wealth, money, and status).

As you go through this chapter, I encourage you to keep Psalm 23:1 in mind. Remember that, in God's eyes, you are already abundant. *The decisions you make in life always determine your outcome,* so it is important to make better and wiser decisions to set yourself up for unimaginable success! This chapter is the light-filled path that God has brought forth to you so you can understand and shift to your soul's content.

The Meaning of Abundance

Many people who are not believers in God's grace may believe that abundance is only determined by how much money they have in their bank account and what their status in society is. But the amount of money in your bank account does not decipher how abundant you truly are. If you are a believer, you will understand the true meaning of what abundance is and how it shows up in your life.

The first time I noticed the difference between myself, who lived in poverty most of my life, and people who had more money than us and lived in better neighborhoods, was when I was sent to an all-white school in the suburbs. I was in the third grade. The segregated school I was in could no longer accommodate a gifted child such as myself, so I needed to take the bus to my new school. It was there that I learned the difference between racism, poverty, affluence, and what I have versus what I don't have. Everything about the white neighborhoods was immaculate—the school, the library, the teachers. The library seemed to have every book an elementary school child could want, and no one needed to share books. The teacher was super nice, in a June Cleaver kind of way.

When I returned home at the end of the school day, it was obvious how different my family and I were from the rest of the world. We were poor; we certainly were not white or privileged.

Knowing and fully understanding this, the only question that surfaced in my mind was *why*. Why was I poor? Why was I living in constant scarcity? Why can't I live like the ones I went to school with? I believed I was just as good as anyone else and I refused to let anyone make me feel less than them, so from that moment on, I decided to choose abundance in every form I could get, not just from money and wealth, but abundance of spirit. Abundance with God and His heavenly kingdom.

Understanding this meaning of abundance led to so many greater blessings.

What Is an Abundant Life?

Living an abundant life means living with the Fruit of the Spirit. Even before we were born, God promised us an extraordinary life. He died on the cross so we can be saved, and we can live exceedingly alongside Him in His kingdom.

So many people believe that living abundantly means the more money in our bank account, the better. If we are making lots of money and have a beautiful house on the hill, we are living abundantly. But God's word doesn't say this. If you exalt Him first, He will bless you abundantly with all the riches you need. Remember Matthew 6:33? "But seek first his kingdom and his righteousness, and all these things will be given to you as well" (*NIV*, 2011/1973).

Of course, you can have all these things, but I encourage you to understand that it is important to acknowledge Jesus Christ in gratitude for all the things you already have so He can continue to bless you with more abundance every single day. If you have your house on the hill, but you believe that you achieved it by your human strength alone, how would it be possible for you to receive more? In Chapter Three, we will be discussing the importance of humility and letting go of pride and ego so we can live an abundant life in all the ways God has offered us.

To truly live an abundant life, there are three concepts we need to understand:

How Does the Bible Define Abundance?

Two words: Exceedingly more. God's promises for a multitude of abundance are evident in many verses in the New Testament.

- **Philippians 4:19**—And my God will meet all your needs according to the riches of his glory in Christ Jesus.

- **Proverbs 3:10**—Then your barns will be filled to overflowing, and your vats will brim over with new wine.

- **Psalms 37:11**—But the meek will inherit the land and enjoy peace and prosperity.

- **Romans 15:13**—May the God of hope fill you with all joy and peace as you trust in him, so that you may overflow with hope by the power of the Holy Spirit.

- **2 Corinthians 9:8**—And God is able to bless you abundantly, so that in all things at all times, having all that you need, you will abound in every good work.

- **John 10:10**—The thief comes only to steal and kill and destroy; I have come that they may have life, and have it to the full.

All these verses, and there are *many* others, speak of the abundant life God offers. When you think of living an abundant life with the Lord, think of it like this: If you exalt Him and praise Him for your continuous blessings, God will bless you with the most abundant life you can ever imagine for yourself. That is His promise.

Living Abundantly Means So Much More Than Wealth and Status

Those who believe that abundance is only defined by wealth, security, and status still have a lot to learn. There are so many people in this world who believe they are living an abundant life and they have less than 100 dollars to their name.

Based on what it says in the scriptures, if abundance was all about money, wealth, and riches, then God would have surely been monetarily rich. But he wasn't. In the eyes of society, Jesus was poor, but in the eyes of the Spirit, He was abundant beyond measure.

In the Bible, Jesus says, "Foxes have dens and birds have nests, but the Son of Man has no place to lay his head" (*NIV*, 2011/1973, Matthew 8:20). This, however, did not stop Jesus from living a fulfilling, abundant life. He gave to the poor, He healed those who were sick, and He sacrificed His life for all mankind so they can live their own abundant life.

When it comes to security, we are secure in Jesus' arms, we are safe for all eternity. Remember that God gives us all that we need every day, we are wealthy. And we are living an abundant life, regardless of what is in our bank account or the type of house or car we have, our status in God's kingdom is immeasurable.

We Will Have an Eternal, Abundant Life with God by Our Side

Trust in the LORD with all your heart and lean not on your own understanding. –
Proverbs 3:5

The moment we lift our life up to God and we believe we are saved, eternity with Him is promised to us, regardless of our social status or the material items we possess. As humans, we may not fully believe we are living an abundant life, but if we accept Jesus Christ as our Savior, we will live in extraordinary abundance in His heavenly kingdom. Living abundantly means eternal life.

We may not understand abundance in its full scope, but just as it states in Proverbs 3:5, it is important we have trust and faith in the Lord and in all that He provides to us. God blesses us abundantly and fervently every single day; understanding this can help guide us onto the path of eternal life with Him in the spiritual realm.

Now this is eternal life: that they know you, the only true God, and Jesus Christ, whom you have sent. –John 17:3

What Is Abundance?

Merriam-Webster describes abundance as all sorts of things: an ample quantity; profusion; affluence; wealth; plentifulness (2023).

Just as we've been stating throughout this chapter thus far, abundance is the ability to believe that we have more than enough every single day. An abundance of health, food, love, support, trust, confidence, spirituality, faith, and money—all of these can constitute the meaning of abundance. We can even have an abundance of gratitude; the point is that there is no wrong answer when it comes to understanding how abundant we are in our lives.

A few of the synonyms that relate to the word abundance are as follows:

- bushel
- loads
- multiplicity
- boatload
- plentitude
- volume
- myriad
- bundle
- heap
- mass

- oodles

- truckload

We can say that we have an abundance of food even though we only have $100 in our bank account. We can also say that we abundantly believe in God and feel richer in spirit and in faith than our neighbor who is an unhappy millionaire. Abundance is about deciphering what it means for our lives and extrapolating it so that we will always feel and remain abundantly happy.

Asking God for the Fruit of the Spirit

The fruit of the Spirit is love, joy, peace, patience, kindness, generosity, faithfulness, gentleness, self-control against such there is no law. –Galatians 5:22-23

In the book of Matthew, God says, "Ask and you shall receive." When we speak of the fruits of the spirit, Galatians refers to nine spiritual gifts: love, joy, peace, patience, kindness, generosity, faithfulness, gentleness, and self-control. If we were to translate this into layman's terms, the fruits are the results we produce because of the work and effort we put in.

As believers in Christ, we must work to embody these fruits so we can experience the goodness of God's grace every single day. We'll be able to experience an abundant life because we make every effort to cultivate love, kindness, compassion, and all the other fruits within our personal growth and within the relationships we have with others.

By embodying these fruits, those who are disbelievers can witness how God is working through us and perhaps, one day, become believers themselves.

Let's discuss these fruits in greater detail:

Love

Although this is the most powerful fruit, most people misunderstand what this fruit represents.

In 1 Corinthians 13:4-7, God says this about love:

> Love is patient, love is kind. It does not envy, it does not boast, it is not proud. It does not dishonor others, it is not self-seeking, it is not easily angered, it keeps no record of wrongs. Love does not delight in evil but rejoices with the truth. It always protects, always trusts, always hopes, always perseveres. *(NIV,* 2011/1973)

If we truly acknowledged this fruit within our spirit, there would be no broken marriages, pride, or ego. But as humans, we make mistakes and fail, but that's okay. We can get up and be better at producing love and try again. The whole point is to demonstrate the love that God bears for us so that others can feel His perfect love surrounding them always.

Love one another as I have loved you. –John 13:34

Joy

To experience pure joy is to be happy in any circumstance. When we feel authentic joy, it is often because we can feel God's love surrounding us., Joy is usually experienced when we have overcome a trial or tribulation. Through His love for us, God compels us to persevere in the face of challenges. We thus become resilient through any challenge and come out of it feeling God's absolute protection.

Consider it pure joy, my brothers and sisters, whenever you face trials of many kinds because you know that the testing of your faith produces perseverance. –James 1:1-2

Peace

Every day, we are surrounded by stress, worry, and anxiety. We think about paying the bills and we are constantly in survival mode most of the time. All these thoughts of scarcity can limit the abundance we receive, which in turn, can bring us overwhelming stress. When we feel that way, we lose peace and try to do everything ourselves. Rather than live in harmony, we live in worry.

God reminds us in Romans that "The mind governed by the flesh is death, but the mind governed by the Spirit is life and peace" *(NIV, 2011/1973, Romans 8:6)*.

In other words, when we entertain a scarcity mindset or we allow our limiting beliefs to take control of our life, we are allowing ourselves to be run by our flesh, while also allowing the enemy to take control of our decisions and our mindset. But when we live solely by faith and allow Jesus Christ to intervene in our lives, we can live in peace and harmony. Trust in Him every day, and He will surround you with peace.

I have told you these things, so that in me you may have peace. In this world you will have trouble. But take heart! I have overcome the world. –John 16:33

Patience

Patience is a word that is lost on many people. Most people will do certain things and expect the results right away, but in the bible, God teaches us that patience is important to experience ultimate abundance in our lives.

Be completely humble and gentle; be patient, bearing with one another in love. –
Ephesians 4:1-2

When we're patient, we can experience peace and harmony. God reminds us that everything we do should be for the glory of His kingdom and in due time, we will reap the harvest. "The one who sows to please the Spirit, from the Spirit will reap eternal life. Let us not become weary in doing good, for at the proper time we will reap a harvest if we do not give up" (*NIV*, 2011/1973, Galatians 8-9).

Patience is a beautiful gift that is within our Holy Spirit. With God's strength within us, we can remain steadfast with our goals and dreams, no matter how long it takes and no matter the challenges that arise in the journey.

Kindness

We have been taught kindness since we were young. If you remember, our parents always taught us that we need to be kind to other kids and that by sharing our toys and cookies, we are being kind to them. When we're kind, we receive the same treatment back.

We are taught in Ephesians 2 that we have an eternal place beside the Father in His heavenly kingdom so long as we express kindness to others because He has expressed kindness to us.

And God raised us up with Christ and seated us with him in the heavenly realms in Christ Jesus, in order that in the coming ages he might show the incomparable riches of his grace, expressed in his kindness to us in Christ Jesus. –Ephesians 2:6-7

As we are aware of this, we can be kind both to those around us and to ourselves. Kindness is expressed in our character and the way we present ourselves to the world. If we are always rude or selfish, we will receive the same toward us. But, if we show kindness to others just as God has asked us to do, it speaks highly of our character and will, therefore, be manifested in a more abundant life.

Generosity

Generosity and kindness go hand in hand. When we're kind, we do what we can to give back, be generous, and show compassion toward others.

There are many ways to be generous:

- Mow your neighbor's lawn.
- Donate to charity.
- Help a friend in need.
- Lend an ear to someone who is currently experiencing challenges.
- Offer your smile.
- Make a meal or two for someone who is sick.
- Bring a coffee to your loved one in bed.
- Volunteer your time to those in need.

All these ways can help you become more generous and build your character with kindness. Every time you offer your generosity, the fruit of your Spirit increases and empowers you to better.

With this in mind, we constantly pray for you, that our God may make you worthy of his calling, and that by his power he may bring to fruition your every desire for goodness and your every deed prompted by faith. –2 Thessalonians 11:11

Faithfulness

Having constant faith is probably one of the hardest things to do in our lives. Especially when we are experiencing challenges left, right, and center, our faith tends to be neglected; but it is God's word in 2 Corinthians that says, "Live by faith, not by sight" (*NIV*, 2011/1973, 2 Corinthians 5:7).

As we live by faith, we can have confidence in God's eternal abilities that He will see through every good work that we have done, and that He will bless us with affirming abundance. By having faith, we can allow the Holy Spirit to work through our lives and we can allow God to surround us with His grace and constant love and affection. It is through faith that we find our strength, perseverance, and determination to carry on and move forward, without giving up.

Gentleness

The story of the Pharisees in John 8 beautifully explains gentleness. As Jesus was teaching, the Pharisees brought a woman to him—she was caught committing adultery, and according to the law, adultery is considered a sin. They challenged Jesus, explaining that the woman should be stoned to death because she was in the wrong by sinning. Jesus challenged everyone right back and asked the people who have never sinned to throw stones at her. Of course, no one obliged. Once Jesus and the woman were left alone, he demonstrated his gentleness by telling her to go home and no longer sin (*NIV*, 2011/1973, John 8: 1-11).

In this story, Jesus expressed His gentleness by being kind to the woman and letting her go; even though she had unrightfully sinned. Some people may sin against us, but the Holy Spirit reminds us to be gentle regardless of what they do and how they sin against us. With gentleness comes humility and forgiveness. Just as people may sin against us, and we are gentle with them, we may also sin and regardless of what we've done, God forgives us and continues to be gentle with us.

For if you forgive other people when they sin against you, your heavenly Father will also forgive you. But if you do not forgive others their sins, your Father will not forgive your sins. –Matthew 6:14-15

Self-Control

Do not conform to the pattern of this world, but be transformed by the renewing of your mind. Then you will be able to test and approve what God's will is—his good, pleasing and perfect will. –Romans 12:2

This is a powerful fruit we need to cultivate within our spirit every single day. Self-control helps us let go of temptation and respond better to situations rather than negatively react to them.

We are all given choices in this life. Jesus died on the cross so that we can be born again and have the power to live above sin by giving us the free will to make our own choices. By choosing wisely, we can practice self-control.

We can also practice self-control by exhibiting faithfulness and patience. We may want things done right away, but it is important to relinquish control to God so He can do the good works within us. By faith and patience, we know His will is already done.

For God gave us a spirit not of fear but of power and love and self-control. –2 Timothy 1:7

Embodying the Fruit of the Spirit

When learning to embody all nine fruits of the spirit, it is important we learn to live as stated in Romans 12:

> Love must be sincere. Hate what is evil; cling to what is good. Be devoted to one another in love. Honor one another above yourselves. Never be lacking in zeal, but keep your spiritual fervor, serving the Lord. Be joyful in hope, patient in affliction,

faithful in prayer. Share with the Lord's people who are in need. Practice hospitality.

Bless those who persecute you; bless and do not curse. Rejoice with those who rejoice; mourn with those who mourn. Live in harmony with one another. Do not be proud but be willing to associate with people in low positions. Do not be conceited.

Do not repay anyone evil for evil. Be careful to do what is right in the eyes of everyone. If it is possible, as far as it depends on you, live at peace with everyone. Do not take revenge, my dear friends, but leave room for God's wrath, for it is written: "It is mine to avenge; I will repay," says the Lord.

"If your enemy is hungry, feed him; if he is thirsty, give him something to drink. In doing this, you will heap burning coals on his head." Do not be overcome by evil but overcome evil with good. (*NIV*, 2011/1973, 9-21)

So how do these verses pertain to this chapter? In what follows, we are exploring how to live an extraordinarily abundant life as a believer. These verses show that to do this, we must conform to the spirit. We must learn to embody the fruits of the spirit that God grows in us so we can righteously live life. By faith, we will succeed, and these verses show us how to do just that.

We should not express love if it is not authentic, otherwise, we are lying to ourselves. When we express love to others, it must be raw, real, genuine, and unique. When we want to experience joy, we should embrace patience, faithfulness, and peace. We cannot have pure joy without experiencing peace, and we cannot have peace without expanding our faith. Thus, we are reminded, to experience true abundance, the fruits of the spirit must be embodied together, otherwise, abundance will not last.

Choosing and Attracting an Abundance Mindset

In all reality, abundance is not hard to cultivate. Attracting an abundant mindset is not hard to achieve. As we've been speaking throughout this chapter, having an abundant mindset is a choice. It's part of the freedom that God has given us. Every single choice that we make can be significantly affected by the way that we think. If we have limiting beliefs about money, we stay in a scarcity mindset, and every decision we take toward our finances will be directed by this mindset.

As I shared in the beginning, I had a choice to stay in a scarcity mindset or to get out of it and step into an abundant one. I could've chosen to continually feel poor and broke and have my decisions reflect this mentality—" I can't afford that." "I never have any money." "I never have enough money." "Why can't I do that?" "What makes them better than me?" But I chose differently. I chose to attract an abundant mindset rather than stick with the scarcity mindset I've been dealt with since childhood, and I became a millionaire in the process.

I'm not saying it's easy to make that switch just like that, as it does take some work, but it is not impossible.

Abundance Mindset Versus Scarcity Mindset

In short, having a scarcity mindset equals having a victim mentality. Those who believe nothing good will ever happen to them have a scarcity mindset. They usually say things such as:

"I can never have that."

"There's not enough for me."

"My life would be perfect if…"

"I will never be able to afford that."

"I am not worthy to achieve that."

"I don't have enough knowledge, expertise, or money to achieve that goal."

They play the victim card. They believe they will never be able to move forward or achieve their goals because they don't have enough of something. It could be money, time, knowledge, or strength—what they currently have never felt enough.

Having a scarcity mindset usually appeals to a lack mindset. Nothing they have will ever be enough. They need more. "When I have that, I will finally be happy and feel abundant." "When I finally go on that vacation, I will feel joy. I will feel like I have finally *made it*." But here's the thing about this statement—you can achieve anything you want in the world, but if you remain in a scarcity mindset, anything you have will never feel enough. You'll keep wanting more, and therefore, you'll be stuck in a scarcity mindset.

Abundant mindset, however, is completely the opposite. You are content with all that you have, no matter how small or big it may be. You look forward to having goals and finding ways to achieve them. You strive to be better and more capable.

Those with an abundant mindset speak these words:

"I am so grateful for everything that I have."

"I love my life as it is right now."

"I trust in God, no matter what."

"I have many things to be grateful for."

"I love my family unconditionally and support them, no matter what."

Those with an abundant mindset seek to expand their outlook on life. They become intentionally aware of all the abundance that currently surrounds them and they feel grateful for it all.

Even though you may not have all that you want right now, it is important to express gratitude for all the things you do have. When gratitude becomes a strong part of your character, you venture on a path toward an abundant mindset.

The Benefits of an Abundant Mindset

There are many benefits to having an abundant mindset:

- You become a role model for God's work within your spirit.

- Your self-awareness is enhanced as you notice the abundance that surrounds you.

- Your faith and trust in God become stronger.

- You become more intentional with what you are doing and who you are.

- You see your life experiences as an extraordinary journey where you've had the opportunity to learn and grow mentally and spiritually.

- You become equipped with the strength you need to push forward through challenges by putting on the armor of God (NIV, 2011/1973, Romans 6:10-17).

Attracting Abundance Into Your Life

In the following chapters, I will explain some of the strategies that I used to go from living a life of poverty for many years to acquiring a net worth of 1.5 million dollars, so keep reading. In the meantime, however, here are some steps you can take to attract abundance into your life.

Gratitude

Despite your current circumstances, it is important to maintain an attitude of gratitude—no pity parties and no feeling sorry for yourself. Remember that there is probably someone else who is worse off than you. Express gratitude for every single thing that you have right now. Say thank you to the people who offer their help, and express gratitude for their time and service. When you can be in a grateful state every day, abundance begins to flow to you, and you become more aware.

Dream It

Whatever you dream, you can achieve—this is not just a slogan. Sit down every day or evening and simply dream. Where do you want to go? What do you want to do? What experiences do you want to have? How much money do you want to make?

I had a very vivid imagination as a child. I held on to it into adulthood, and it came to fruition. People may feel that your dreams are impossible. Do not allow their beliefs to influence the way you feel. Keep dreaming. Don't stop.

Alter Your Mindset

Instead of focusing on what you don't have, focus on what you do have. When attracting an abundant mindset, it is important to eliminate as much negativity as possible so you can alter your mindset seamlessly. This includes toxic people, places, and environments that are negative. When you focus on the positive aspects of life, it will bring you more of what you want to have in your life. And that is like money in the bank.

Stop Making Excuses

Every human being on the planet has something going on in their lives—work, business, family, life transitions, personal growth—there is always an opportunity to make excuses as to why we are not further along in our lives than we currently are. Learn to rise above your situation. When Nike coined the slogan *Just Do It,* that is exactly what they meant, urging you to follow your dreams. Do the things that make you feel abundant and do not allow any excuses to get in your way. Mistakes will happen and that's okay. Keep your focus on your goals, learn from your mistakes, and eventually you will win.

Realize Your Potential

Write a personal resume of all your accomplishments. This is a tried-and-true mindset-altering exercise that will remind you of the value you bring to the table. When you're not feeling worthy or enough, this personal resume will encourage you and remind you of all the blessings that God has given you up until now. When I am feeling unworthy, I read my resume and my bio out loud to myself so that it really sticks in my mind, and I count my blessings and name them one by one and thank God for them.

Do Not Let Opportunities Pass You By

If you make a decision and commit to it, promising yourself that you will do anything to achieve your goals, you have already set yourself up for incredible success. Do not let fear stop you from achieving what you want—go out and get it. God gave Adam and Eve the whole garden to play in, and they let fear in the form of a snake (Satan) cast them out of the garden simply because they were afraid of what they did not know. When you decide what you want, opportunities show up; it is important you become aware of them, so you don't miss your calling. When opportunity presents itself, do not procrastinate or make excuses; learn to trust yourself and have faith that God is working alongside you to make things happen.

Commit to Learning Your Dream

Education, education, education my dear child—ignorance is not bliss in this situation. When you are well prepared for whatever stands before you, it breeds confidence. Find someone who is doing exactly what you want to do and study them. Learn what they're doing and commit to yourself that you will learn all that you can about your dreams. God gives you the vision, so He is obligated to provide the provision, but it is up to you to study, learn, and grow to demonstrate that you are worthy of His provision. Faith without work is futile!

Meditation

To remain steadfast in what I'm referring to in this chapter, I encourage you to meditate on the following verses, some of which I have already quoted throughout this chapter; meditating on them now helps to reinforce your abundance mindset. Allow the verses to soak into your soul so you can gain a spiritual interpretation of how they show up in your life.

- 2 Corinthians 9:8
- John 10:10
- Deuteronomy 28:12
- Ephesians 3:20
- Exodus 34:6
- James 1:17
- Luke 6:38
- Luke 6:45
- Matthew 6:33
- Philippians 4:19
- Proverbs 3:5
- Proverbs 3:10
- Psalms 23:5
- Psalms 36:8
- Psalms 37:11
- Psalms 65:11
- Psalms 72:16
- Romans 15:13
- Psalms 66:8-12
- 1 Timothy 5:8

As there are *many* verses about having an abundant life, I do not expect you to meditate on each one every single day. Choose one, two, or a few, and read up on them. Gather your insight and how it pertains to your life, then consider the shifts you need to make in your mindset. Once you become aware of how they relate to your life, you can move on to a few more verses and do the same thing. Understanding God's message for you in these verses will help you attract an abundant mindset moving forward.

As you know from this chapter, it is important to make that shift from a scarcity mindset to an abundant mindset so you can begin to live in peace, joy, and harmony.

Some of the takeaways you can conclude from this chapter are:

- Abundance is a decision and commitment to yourself.

- You can attract abundance into your life if you stop making excuses, learn from your mistakes, and express gratitude for every little thing you currently have in your life.

- The fruits of the spirit are always within you. As the Holy Spirit surrounds you with Grace, you can awaken the fruits by simple gestures you take in your life.

- Living an abundant life is not impossible; it takes hard work and effort to make it happen. And this starts with a simple decision to choose abundance. Everything else will follow.

Now that you know how to achieve an abundant life, the next chapter will discuss the next steps. We'll be talking about the importance of humility and letting pride and ego go so you can experience joy and happiness. Being humble is one of the most important keys to living abundantly—Chapter Three will show you how to do just that.

Chapter 3:

It Is Not About You

To achieve an abundant life spiritually, emotionally, and financially, the first thing you need to do is to realize that it is not about you. It is never about you.

As a child, I experienced sexual, emotional, and physical abuse. I became a teen mom at 16 years old. As a young woman, I experienced spousal abuse and after two marriages, which both ended in divorce, I was bankrupt in every way possible—spiritually, emotionally, and financially.

When I finally realized that the trauma was not all about me, I began to heal. This is what I learned. To achieve an abundant life through the eyes of the Spirit, the life experiences we go through are meant to happen so we can learn about healing and spiritual restoration.

There was a time when spiritual warfare took control of my life, and I felt suicidal. But while I was praying, the Holy Spirit revealed something to me that was so profound: Nothing that I have gone through was pointless; I had endured the trials I went through because I needed to be a blessing to someone else. The Holy Spirit told me that God would use every circumstance and every situation I experienced for the Glory of His Kingdom. That my overcoming every experience would not be in vain. So live and live free!

One of the first steps to living an abundant life starts with humility. To be honest, being humble seems to be a bit of a lost cause for many people. When we think we have it all made and we feel we don't need God in our life to guide us, this is when we learn. And boy, do we learn!

An important scripture about humility is found In Philippians, "do nothing out of selfish ambition or vain conceit," but rather to do everything humbly (*NIV*, 2011/1973, Philippians 2:3-4). Rather than focus on yourself, focus on caring for and nurturing others. I also like to think of this verse as God speaking about compassion. Of course, some selfish people create their wealth, without turning to God, but in my opinion, doing things with God is so much more rewarding. Remember, this book is for Believers.

I remember a time in my life when I was tired of waiting on God. I told God that He was taking too long and that I was going to do life my way! Can you relate to this? Sometimes our impatience gets the best of us. That's what happened to me.

As soon as I uttered those words, I felt the universe shift. It was then that I met my second husband. Even though I had three children from a previous marriage, we got together and started building a life as one big happy family.

At the time, we both worked at low-income jobs but we both quickly excelled at our professions. My husband worked in an entry-level position in the mailroom, but eventually, he made his way up to become an advertising executive. As for myself, I started as a cashier to pay the bills and eventually became an Associate Programmer Analyst and soon after, a manager of the company.

As for our personal life, my husband, children, and I went from renting a home, getting paid minimum wage, to not only building a home but earning a six-figure income. My children had the best education our city could offer, and we truly enjoyed a lavish lifestyle.

I remember taking my Bible and putting it on the shelf. I didn't open it much. It was seriously collecting dust!

I foolishly thought that I was all that and a bag of chips. Go figure! There wasn't a single humble bone in my body at that moment. I had everything I ever wanted—a marriage, a big house, an excellent career, kids—and I did it all by myself.

You know, it's funny that when you come from poverty, you hang on to every material thing that comes your way. And your unhealthy relationships. You hang onto them as if your life depended on them. I felt unstoppable, but inwardly I was in a shambles. My world was crumbling.

No one knew that my husband was extremely abusive, and my children were unhappy. As I look back, I realize that no amount of money or prestige can ever replace peace of mind or true happiness.

Every day, I was in constant fear that I would lose everything, and guess what? My wish is my command. I did. I remember that night as if it were only yesterday. I got into a car accident with a drunk driver. I almost lost my life. For nine months, I was stuck in a wheelchair, trying to recover. In total, it took me two years to recover physically, but emotionally my life was a mess. My marriage fell apart, my teenage children became rebellious, and financially, I was ruined. I felt like I lost everything. My pride, my drive, my self-love… gone in an instant.

So, you may ask… how did I get from there when I felt my life crumbling down, feeling alone and prideful, to now living abundantly with God always by my side?

I did the following three things:

- I asked God for forgiveness. I should have never thought I could do life without Him. I need Him in my life always.

- I humbled myself and broke down all my pride, and God gave me a new vision for my life.

- I learned to forgive my haters. I learned to not only forgive myself but to accept forgiveness from those who have wronged me.

As you can tell from my story, this chapter focuses on the importance of authentic humility. I say *authentic* because many people pretend to be humble on the outside, but on the inside, they're full of pride and ego.

This chapter is about looking inward and reminding yourself that God wants a humble person. If there is someone to forgive, then find it in your heart to forgive. If you are not sure how to forgive or even accept forgiveness, this chapter will break it down for you, so you understand.

The Virtue of Humility

At some point or another, we've been taught to be humble—by our parents, by the older generation adults in our lives, such as our grandparents, and even by our teachers at school. And sometimes we are taught what not to do in the face of humility when we experience a situation that is beyond our control.

But what does the Lord say about humility? This is what we explore in this chapter. We can follow our parents, grandparents, and teachers when they try to teach us a lesson about staying humble, but we must pay attention to God's words of wisdom when He speaks about humility.

James 4:10 says, "Humble yourselves before the Lord and He will lift you up" (*NIV*, 2011/1973). How do we humble ourselves before the Lord? There are many people who 1) are not sure how to do this, and 2) take it for granted because they believe they can do it all on their own. This is where pride and ego step in; to be truly humble, we must know the difference between pride and humility so we can become aware of when we are acting prideful and then rectify it as such while being obedient to God's word.

This chapter will address the following topics:

- The virtue of humility—the true meaning of humility and what it means to be humble, according to the Bible.

- Joseph's story from Genesis 37 is a lesson in humility and forgiveness at the same time.

- The importance of forgiveness and what it means to forgive others and accept forgiveness.

By the end of the chapter, I trust you will be able to define humility for yourself and formulate your definition as God's word speaks to your heart. I trust you will understand what it truly means to forgive not only yourself for any wrongdoings but forgive others for what they've done to you. This is one of the hardest things to do, but by trusting God, you will find your way, and He will direct your path.

What Is Humility?

According to Merriam-Webster, humility is defined as having the "freedom from pride or arrogance: the quality or state of being humble" (2023).

Now, according to Christianity.com, humility is about "genuine gratitude" (2022). Psalm 25:9 says, "He guides the humble in what is right and teaches them his way" (*NIV*, 2011/1973).

In the bible, we are taught to be humble. We are taught to let go of pride

and ego and serve and forgive, regardless of our circumstances.

As you know from my story, I came from humble beginnings. While my family was on welfare, it taught me to learn to appreciate everything that I have. So, when the government offered their assistance, I was grateful.

Of course, I am also human. I can't say that I was always humble. When I was experiencing childhood abuse, and then my marriages were falling apart, I embraced the victim mentality. I didn't understand why my journey was playing out the way that it did, but eventually, God led me back down the road to humility and righteousness.

I remembered this verse in Proverbs and then my life started to shift.

Trust in the Lord with all your heart and lean not on your own understanding; in all your ways submit to him, and he will make your paths straight. –Proverbs 3:5-6

This verse teaches us that although we may not consciously understand what we're going through, it is important to keep our eye on the Lord; to get back into a humble state because eventually when our pride has been swept away, we will notice that God has brought us back onto a lighted path.

The Importance of Forgiveness

In my story, there were so many times when I could've chosen not to forgive and continue playing the victim. When I was being abused, when my family was living in an impoverished state, when I became a teen mom, when I filed for bankruptcy, when my marriages failed—these were experiences I lived through that rightfully tested my humility, my faith in God, and whether I could forgive those who wronged me and whether I could forgive myself.

Let me just tell you: Forgiveness is not an easy journey. To be honest, it's long and feels lonely every step of the way. It feels as though no one understands what you're going through and that you're meant to live a lonely, dreary, and bitter life. But I should point out that when you do find it in your heart to forgive, you have understood how to fully heal and restore your spirit and confidence.

I have learned that there are a few myths about forgiveness. Trusting these myths is neither godly nor healthy for your self-esteem and healing. But understanding why they're around in the first place will help you understand who you are in Christ Jesus.

- **Forgiving is about forgetting.** I want to make something very clear: Just because you have chosen to forgive does not mean you have forgotten that people have wronged you. It just means that you have found a way to love them again, despite what they have done.

- **People can do whatever they like with you.** You are choosing to forgive because God has asked you to love one another, but it doesn't mean that people can push you around and play with your trust again.

- **You are not allowed to be angry.** In Chapter Five, we'll be speaking about the importance of controlling your emotions. Anger is an important emotion. However, let me be clear: Even though you have chosen to forgive, you are still in the right to be angry and express emotions. It doesn't mean you're a bad person; it simply means you're human and you are learning on this journey, just like everyone else in this world.

- **You need to pretend everything is okay.** Of course, things are not okay. But you are allowing yourself to be open to the possibility that one day, things will happen. You are giving yourself time and space to heal mentally, emotionally, and spiritually. At times, the greatest forgiveness is when you have forgiven in your heart, even though the people involved don't know you have forgiven them.

Ways to Forgive

Once you're on the path of forgiveness, it's going to be a very healing journey. Below are a few ways that can help you find it in your heart to forgive others:

- **Acknowledgement:** Identify what is causing you to lack forgiveness and acknowledge the situation.

- **Acceptance:** It's okay to accept how you feel. You're a spiritual being going through a human experience and you're learning how to navigate this life. By accepting the hurt and shame you feel, you will feel comfortable naming your emotions and expressing them to yourself and to those who have wronged you.

- **Hold your boundaries:** It's powerful to forgive, but that doesn't mean you need to let go of your boundaries, so the situation happens again. It is important to remain steadfast within your boundaries and be mindful of the fact that you are strong, and you know how to handle the situation with courage if you are faced with a similar trial.

- **Learn when you're in the wrong:** When you're forgiving someone, it is important to also hold yourself accountable. If you want them to apologize, find it in your heart to acknowledge the fact that you have also hurt them. Playing the victim never serves anyone.

- **Let go and let God:** Understand why you experienced this journey in the first place. Ask God to help you forgive. Seek His guidance so that He may comfort you in times of suffering. Bring your forgiveness up to God and allow Him to work through your spirit.

- **Trust that it all happened for a reason:** Although the situation hurt you, understand why it needed to happen. Did the situation make you stronger, more resilient, empathetic, or compassionate? Allow all the spiritual reasons to come forward as understanding them helps you trust the Lord's will for your life. You don't need to stay in the trauma. You can reframe your story so that it becomes a part of your purpose to help others.

Forgiving your haters or those who harmed you does not mean that God is about to let them go unpunished. Many scriptures can attest to this fact. I can say from my experience that I have seen how God dealt with those people who did me harm. Forgiving allows you to release bitterness and anger.

To be frank, if I had taken matters into my own hands, I would be authoring this book from a prison cell. Forgiving a perpetrator does not mean that you let someone who has abused you get away with it. On the contrary, if you or someone you know is being abused, you must report them to the authorities and seek help. You do not have to endure abuse to be loved.

But to you who are listening I say: Love your enemies, do good to those who hate you. –Luke 6:27

Whoever conceals their sins does not prosper, but the one who confesses and renounces them finds mercy. –Proverbs 28:13

Joseph's Story

So, you may know the bible story of Joseph and his brothers. If you are not familiar with it, here is how it goes:

Joseph was one of Jacob's 12 sons. His father loved him more than any of the others and gave him a colored cloak. His brothers were jealous of him, and because of this jealousy, they sold him into slavery.

Joseph went through many trials while in Egypt, but eventually, he was promoted to a prominent position. When there was a famine, Joseph's family came to Egypt for food. They did not recognize him because it had been many years since they had seen him, and on top of that, his brothers told their father that Joseph was dead. When Joseph realized that it was his family that stood before him needing help, he chose to help them, despite the wrongdoings his brothers caused him. He learned to forgive his brothers and chose to help, despite what had happened. You can read more about Joseph in Genesis 37-50.

The point of the story is that God is the Judge. It is not within our right to judge and condemn others, because God will do this. We can love them and find a way to forgive them. God will do the rest.

Forgiving Yourself and Accepting Forgiveness

When we make mistakes, we must learn to forgive ourselves. I know this is easier said than done, but when learning to forgive ourselves, we need to remember what it says in Ephesians 4: "Be kind and compassionate to one another, forgiving each other, just as in Christ God forgave you" (*NIV*, 2011/1973, Ephesians 4:32).

If we were to break this verse down, it reiterates compassion toward others as well as to ourselves. Showing ourselves grace and compassion is a big step toward self-forgiveness. It's not easy to be kind to ourselves, especially if we make a mistake. We bully ourselves and tear ourselves down. But if we remember that Christ has already forgiven us of any wrongdoings, just as it is said in Ephesians 4, we can take the steps toward healing and self-forgiveness.

When you learn self-forgiveness, there are a few things that can happen.

- You learn to accept what you did.
- Chances are, you'll experience remorse, guilt, or shame.

- You'll feel apologetic and wonder where things went wrong and what you can do to regain your self-trust and confidence.

- You may want to talk to others about what happened. Maybe even confess what you did or talk to the other parties involved.

- You may write a journal about the situation or write a forgiveness letter about the situation to understand the emotions you're feeling.

A few of these steps can help when learning to forgive yourself, especially when you take the time to write a forgiveness letter to yourself. There is something very healing about this exercise. You can express every single emotion you're feeling in the letter so you can find a way to patch things up with your self-trust. Writing this letter not only helps you heal, but it helps you increase your mental health, so your negative emotions decrease.

When we don't forgive ourselves, we can go down a very dark path. We can get depressed, our anxiety can skyrocket, and we may even be suicidal. When finding a way to forgive ourselves, we can decrease these symptoms and remind ourselves that God loves us, despite our wrongdoings. We will no longer feel anxious, but instead, we will feel comforted by God's unconditional love.

Benefits of Self-Forgiveness

Forgiving ourselves has many benefits, such as the following:

- increased self-compassion
- healing and restoration
- decreased anxiety
- positive mindset
- more calm and peace

- rejuvenated spirit

- more focus

- deeper connection to God

- deeper connection to self

- more self-love

- increased self-confidence and trust

- resilience and determination to make a change

- self-acceptance

If we absolutely cannot find it in our hearts to forgive ourselves, it could be for a few reasons:

- **We don't believe anything is wrong.** In other words, our pride gets in the way, and we don't feel there is anything we need to forgive ourselves for.

- **Our self-worth is non-existent.** We are so deep down a dark path that we don't feel we are worthy of forgiveness. This is because we forgot who we are. We may be a child of God, but in our mind, we are not worthy to be loved by anyone, let alone be worthy of forgiving ourselves.

- **We tell ourselves we will never heal.** In Chapter Eight, we speak about affirmations, which are positive, empowering statements. In this case, telling ourselves that we will never heal sounds like the opposite of an affirmation. We are affirming to ourselves that we don't deserve to heal, and therefore, we don't deserve to forgive ourselves.

- **We are concerned by what other people think rather than what God thinks of us.** Many times, we fear judgment from others, so we may think that if we try to forgive ourselves, others may judge our choices and feel we're in the wrong. I encourage you to stop looking outside for answers and start looking within.

We hold the spirit of God, which means we are always filled with light. We must learn to focus on the love of God within us, rather than the judgment that may fall before us.

When you do not forgive yourself, you become self-destructive and try to mask the pain you feel. This can lead to addiction, such as drugs, food, pornography, drinking, and promiscuity —these are all excuses just to numb the pain. They are temporary distractions that can steer you away from God's love and into Satan's arms. By forgiving ourselves, we release all that retribution and persecution, and we remember that Christ has already won our battles.

As you learn to forgive yourself, I want you to remember something: You are worthy of forgiveness. Accepting that forgiveness is challenging as we tend to beat ourselves up unmercifully. Do not allow others to degrade you or hold your sins against you. People will always try to remind you of where you came from to make you feel like you do not deserve all the blessings that have come your way. Don't listen. Instead, focus on the love of Christ that surrounds you. Focus on the joy and peace of being in His arms; He is your Father, your protector, your guide.

I learned that by telling my story, I was reaping coals of fire on my enemy's head. For all the people who think that you will never amount to anything or put stumbling blocks in your way, I encourage you to use the experiences that have happened to you for the betterment of someone else. This could be your way of serving others—honor it. Not only will you achieve success, but you will accomplish what the bible says in Proverbs 25:22: "For thou shalt heap coals of fire upon his head, and the Lord shall reward thee" (KJV, 2021/1611, Proverbs 25:22). Remember, living well, full of fruitfulness and humility, is always the best revenge.

Meditation

As you navigate your path to forgiveness, I encourage you to meditate on the following verses. These passages will help give you clarity and restore your spirit:

- Psalm 103:12

- Ephesians 1:7

- 1 John 1:9

- Daniel 9:9

- Micah 7:18-19

- Luke 5:20

- Luke 6:37

- Colossians 3:13

- Ephesians 4:31-32

- Matthew 6:9-15

As you learn to forgive yourselves, you start to free your mind of any negative thoughts—a process we discuss at length in the next chapter.

However, before we move on to Chapter Four, here are a few highlights I'd like you to remember from this chapter:

- It is important to focus on being humble and serving the Lord as much as you can.

- Always remember where you've come from—consider it your humble beginnings.

- Even though you may have sinned, remember that Christ has already forgiven you.

- Learn to let go of pride and ego so you can fully embrace humility.

- Self-forgiveness brings many benefits, such as healing, restoration, and compassion.

- Accepting forgiveness is not an easy feat, but it is not impossible.

- Learning to forgive yourself and others takes time.

I encourage you to remind yourself of these points as you begin to read Chapter Four. Our mind can be full of self-destructing thoughts—forgiving ourselves and showing compassion to ourselves can be the start of freeing our mind. Chapter Four will show you how to do just that.

Chapter 4:

Free Your Mind and the Rest Will Follow

God gave us the freedom to do what we want and make the choices that will lead to an abundant life. Now, let's remember: To achieve an abundant life, we must put God at the center of our decisions.

Free your mind, and the rest will follow is a lyric from one of my favorite songs, Free Your Mind, by En Vogue. It speaks about racism and inequality, but the truth of the statement applies to anything we may do in life. When you make the decision to free your mind, everything else—abundance, goals, dreams, results—will follow suit.

One of my favorite books that has also helped me was *Battlefield of the Mind*, by Joyce Meyers. This book discusses ways to overcome confusion, anger, depression, and negative thoughts because low and behold, the battlefield is the mind.

Every time we experience a negative situation, what happens? Our mind holds onto it and replays it over and over, like a broken record player. If you truly want to achieve abundance, it is necessary to do what you can to free your mind of any toxic thoughts.

In all fairness, achieving money or status does not make you a happy or content person; on the contrary, it can keep you stuck in a scarcity mindset, and even though you may have lots of money to last you a lifetime, you will always feel like you don't have enough. Your mind will tell you so, and you'll believe it. Learning to free your mind will free you of any toxicity in and around you. By constantly having negative thoughts, you block your path to abundance.

The Bible says in Romans 12:

> Therefore, I urge you, brothers, and sisters, in view of God's mercy, to offer your bodies as a living sacrifice, holy and pleasing to God—this is your true and proper worship. Do not conform to the pattern of this world but be transformed by the renewing of your mind. Then you will be able to test and approve what God's will is—his good, pleasing and perfect will. (*NIV*, 2011/1973, 1-2)

The steps to renewing and freeing your mind will not happen overnight; I wish this was the case, but God asks us to do the work to glorify His kingdom. This is a continuous journey, one that is done daily so we can hold ourselves accountable for the outcome. Freeing your mind takes consistent effort and the spiritual desire to change. When we put God at the center of our life, things happen. Abundance happens. Our mindset is renewed and restored.

To encourage you, here are a few steps you can put in place right away that will help free your mind from any toxicity you're experiencing. To truly transform your life, it is important you act—these steps will help move you forward in the right direction.

Ask the Lord to Make Your Path Straight

As we've discussed in Romans 12:2, transformation begins by renewing our minds. There is no doubt that every single decision that we make is based on the thoughts and beliefs that come from our minds. If our mind is full of negativity, our decisions, and the actions we take will be based on how we feel in that moment. Many people, unless this is fully understood, can go for numerous years embracing a scarcity mindset and negative thoughts without realizing that this mentality is affecting their decision-making.

If you're one of these people, you are encouraged to seek God's wisdom in this case. Ask Him to help make your path straight, and to direct your mind so that it focuses on abundance rather than scarcity. Ask Him to guard your thoughts and beliefs so that they no longer have a negative influence on your decisions, and that you may feel free to live an abundant life, full of joy, peace, and happiness. Ask the Lord to protect your mind from negative people and environments so that their energy doesn't affect the way you think about yourself or create beliefs that don't serve you.

Become Aware of Negative Thoughts: Where Do They Come From?

The enemy will do anything he can to destroy you and find a way to bring you closer to him rather than focus your attention on God's will for your life. Usually, that means he will try to attack you through your mind, making you think and believe things that are not true. It's his feeble attempt at gaining access to your soul. If you allow it because you feel you are weak, you may have many self-defeating thoughts that greatly affect your decisions as well as your ability to control what you do.

I have learned that the way to fight this is through Prayer and Scripture. In cases such as this, where spiritual warfare is imminent, positive self-talk or talking yourself out of something is not enough. It is important you understand that you can only fight the enemy with Prayer and God's Word.

The Bible says in Ephesians 6:11-12,

> Put on the full armor of God, so that you can take your stand against the devil's schemes. For our struggle is not against flesh and blood, but against the rulers, against the authorities, against

the powers of this dark world and against the spiritual forces of evil in the heavenly realms. (*NIV*, 2011/1973)

When I was a child, I was blessed to attend Sunday school with my grandmother. I did not realize how much I had learned about the Bible in Sunday school and church until I was going through my healing process. Scriptures that I had learned from memory or just osmosis would come to my mind, which caused me to pull out my old dusty Bible.

When a negative thought would enter my mind or a bad memory had me gripped in fear and panic, I would read the Bible out loud. I have learned and experienced what Proverbs 18 states: "The tongue has the power of life and death, and those who love it will eat its fruit" (*NIV*, 2011/1973, Proverbs 18:21).

So, speak *life* into your situation, knowing that God's Word is not just ink on a page, but it is alive.

The Bible states in Hebrew 4:

> For the word of God is alive and active. Sharper than any double-edged sword, it penetrates even to divide soul and spirit, joints, and marrow; it judges the thoughts and attitudes of the heart. Nothing in all creation is hidden from God's sight. Everything is uncovered and laid bare before the eyes of him to whom we must give account. (*KJV*, 2021/1611, Hebrews 4:12)

When these thoughts feel overpowering, it is important that you seek the love of Christ even more so that you can feel His presence in your life, even when things feel difficult to overcome.

Understanding where these self-defeating thoughts and limiting beliefs come from will help you cut ties from the source (aka the enemy) so that you can move forward more positively. Remember that your battles have already been won and that God is always in control. He will always stand with you, strong and affirmed, regardless of whether you fully seek Him or not.

At times, you may go through spiritual warfare in your mind. You feel you can't do something or you're not strong enough to overcome your battles but remembering that God is faithful will help bring peace into your heart, despite any enemy attacks.

Let Go of Self-Defeating Thoughts and Replace Them With a God-Focused Mindset

Do not conform to the patterns of this world…

As we pray for our paths to be straight and as we become aware of negative thoughts and enemy attacks, we can align ourselves to a God-focused mindset. Rather than entertain the thoughts and beliefs of this world, we can focus on how God wants to work through our lives and the mission He has for us on this earth.

I understand that focusing solely on God may not be easy, but with time, our thoughts and beliefs will align with the Holy Spirit. In all fairness, I feel it's better to put our faith and trust in God alone instead of putting our faith in the humans of this world and trying to do everything all on our own. Of course, this may feel like a struggle because you can 100% put your faith in God and His protection, but since you're living a human experience on this earth, it is up to you to make the right decisions and take the appropriate actions that benefit God's work and not the enemy.

If this feels like a difficult task, I want to encourage you with these verses from Colossians 3: "If then you have been raised with Christ, seek the things that are above, where Christ is, seated at the right hand of God. Set your minds on things that are above, not on things that are on earth" (*NIV*, 2011/1973, Colossians 3:1-3).

If you watched the movie *Gone with the Wind,* based on Margaret Mitchell's novel, one of my favorite lines by Scarlett O'Hara, as played by Vivien Leigh, was, "I won't think about that today, if I think about that I'll go crazy, and I won't think about that now I'll think about that tomorrow because tomorrow is another day."

She was good at staying in the moment, regardless of what was going on around her; good or bad, she stayed focused on the task ahead.

We, as Believers, must stay focused whenever we are feeling oppressed, or our mind takes us back to a painful memory. I encourage you to ask God to release you from sorrowful memories and focus on these scriptures:

- "For his anger lasts only a moment, but his favor lasts a lifetime; weeping may stay for the night, but rejoicing comes in the morning" (*NIV,* 2011/1973, Psalm 30:5)

- "If then you have been raised with Christ, seek the things that are above, where Christ is, seated at the right hand of God. Set your minds on things that are above, not on things that are on earth (*NIV,* 2011/1973, Colossians 3:1-2).

- "For those who live according to the flesh set their minds on the things of the flesh, but those who live according to the Spirit set their minds on the things of the Spirit" (*NIV,* 2011/1973, Romans 8:5)

- "Finally, brothers, whatever is true, whatever is honorable, whatever is just, whatever is pure, whatever is lovely, whatever is commendable, if there is any excellence, if there is anything worthy of praise, think about these things" (*NIV,* 2011/1973, Philippians 4:8).

Jesus Accepts You, No Matter What

The Poet Menander said, "Time heals all wounds" around 300 BC, and that remains true today. You will get to a place of peace and acceptance that will restore your soul.

I've learned that the only way to have peace in my mind is to understand and remember that Jesus accepts me, no matter what I've done and who I am. I could be rich or poor, black, or white, short, or tall—in God's eyes, just as it says in Genesis, I am created in the likeness and image of Him, and I am perfect just the way I am. I can rest in the spiritual truth of knowing that my acceptance in the heavenly realm is confirmed and approved by God Himself, and I don't need to seek approval from any human on this earth.

This also goes for you too. Take comfort in knowing you don't need to seek approval and acceptance from anyone but God who always accepts and loves you just the way you are.

In Roman 8, Jesus declares that "we are free from condemnation" (*NIV*, 2011/1973, Romans 8:1) and, further along, that "we are His children" (*NIV*, 2011/1973, Romans 8:16-17) Just as our earthly parents accept us exactly the way we are, so too we can be certain that our Heavenly Father accepts us, no matter what.

Practical Steps to Healing

Clinical Depression is a Mood Disorder. You cannot just snap out of it.

The sign of clinical depression is a "persistent feeling of sadness or loss of interest" that "can lead to a range of behavioral and physical symptoms. These may include sleep, appetite, energy level, concentration, daily behavior, or self-esteem changes. Depression can also be associated with thoughts of suicide" (American Academy of Clinical Psychology, n.d.).

If you feel you are experiencing clinical depression, I encourage you to seek medical attention or contact 911. I want to be clear—there is no shame in seeking help. It will speak very highly of you and your desire to get better mentally, emotionally, and spiritually.

Speaking to a counselor can also help you navigate your feelings, as a counseling session will allow you to talk with an objective person who is not emotionally involved in your situation. The counselor will help you release any toxic feelings toward yourself, others, or a situation so that you can feel free to be yourself. In a session, there is no judgment or condemnation; the counselor is there to listen to you and offer professional support and expertise.

I also want to share that writing has saved my life. I encourage you to journal daily about your feelings and emotions. Journaling allows you to free your mind by putting your thoughts on paper, especially when you cannot speak to another person. It allows you to be yourself without judgment, ridicule from others, or negative feedback.

Think of journaling as a secret best friend whose only job is to listen to you. Listen to what you must share, the feelings you're experiencing, and the thoughts that are going through your mind. I have noticed that journaling has *huge* healing benefits. Here are a few:

- It offers you clarity.
- It helps you increase your self-esteem and confidence.
- It helps you voice your thoughts to someone who truly needs to hear them: you.
- It helps you become more self-aware.
- It offers you more peace every time you write and reduces stress, worry, and fear.

- It helps you understand yourself better.

Lather, Rinse, Repeat

Practice makes perfect, and reaching a place of peace takes work. One of my favorite quotes by Lao Tzu says it all: "Watch your thoughts, they become your words; watch your words, they become your actions; watch your actions, they become your habits; watch your habits, they become your character; watch your character, it becomes your destiny."

Creating a daily practice when focusing on working on these steps takes hard work, dedication, and commitment. For example, when wanting to work out to tone and shape your body, it is important to understand a few things:

- Why you're doing it.

- How strongly you desire to tone your body.

- How committed you will be.

- The things that can stop you from achieving your goals.

When you know the answers to all these questions, you'll have clarity, which in turn, can help you progress and succeed. If you're not sure why you're wanting to tone your body in the first place, your goals are as good as dead.

This is the same for following these steps to transform your mind. If you're not sure why you want to shift your mind, your commitment and dedication to your transformation will be non-existent. Later, you wonder why you're still in the same boat of a scarcity mindset. It's because you weren't fully committed–that's why you haven't experienced any positive results.

With any transformation, it takes consistent action to experience results. I encourage you to repeat these four steps over and over again daily, so you are constantly reminded of God's unconditional love and affection.

Whenever you feel down or feel like you're having difficulty overcoming a challenge, acting on these steps will encourage you to move forward, knowing you are covered by God's grace and healing. Just as we are reminded in Romans, Jesus will never condemn you, so you can be certain that you can make mistakes and learn from them without being reprimanded by God. He protects you, your thoughts, and your beliefs from the enemy every single day; it is up to you to be open to God's will for your life and allow the Holy Spirit to work through, cleanse, and heal your mind so you can be renewed.

Meditation

To truly free your mind from any toxicity that is clogging it up, I encourage you to meditate on the following verses. They help give you clarity on what you need to do to focus solely on God. Just as with the previous meditations, focus on a couple, trying to understand how they pertain to your life before moving on to the others.

- Matthew 6:33
- Psalms 1:1-6
- Romans 8:5
- Philippians 4:8
- Matthew 6:24
- Proverbs 2:2-5
- Colossians 2:6-8
- 2 Timothy 3:16-17

- Hebrews 12:1-2

- 1 Peter 2:1-25

- Romans 12:9

- Isaiah 26:3

Every single day, our mind goes through a variety of emotions. And every single day, we process about 70,000 thoughts! (Cleveland Clinic, 2015) We've learned from this chapter that we have the choice to free our minds anytime we want. If you're experiencing debilitating thoughts daily, I encourage you to follow the steps I detailed in this chapter so that you can release what no longer serves you and replace those thoughts with those of abundance.

Some of the key points we can highlight from this chapter are:

- Jesus accepts you exactly as you are, no matter what you look like and what you do.

- Becoming aware of self-defeating thoughts can help you understand the root cause of where they come from so you can cut them off at the source. Remember, God is in control, always.

- Praying to the Lord and asking Him to direct your path and guard your mind can help bring you more peace and abundance.

- To achieve an abundant life, it is important to replace the toxic thoughts with a God-focused mindset, knowing that you are God's children.

This chapter provides a beautiful segue into the next chapter that will be walking you through how to manage your emotions daily, so you are no longer controlled by negative emotions, but rather you experience feelings of abundance.

Chapter 5:

Get Your Emotions, Get Your Life

When I relocated from Boston, Massachusetts to California, I was going through my first divorce. So many emotions were running through me in these moments. I felt angry, disillusioned, and bitter. I was raised to have a fairy-tale marriage. My marriage, which was a Christian marriage, was supposed to last forever–so long as I did my part of being the submissive, dutiful, loving wife.

I believed my ex when he made the promise to love, honor, cherish, and respect me.

Well, folks, that didn't happen. We were together for 10 years and then we weren't for reasons that I will not explain in this book; but let's just say that after much prayer, God finally gave me the go-ahead to move on my own. His confirmation came from Psalms 37. I packed up my children and I moved to California, just like the Beverly Hillbillies, but I hadn't struck gold yet!

It was during those challenging times that I needed to learn to deal with my anger issues and my emotions. I learned something so profound during these moments. I was responsible for taking control of my life. Not my family, not my ex-husband, not my friends, associates, or co-workers... just me. I learned that if I genuinely wanted to be successful and have the abundant life that God promised me, I had to learn to get my emotions in check.

I could not walk around carrying everything I felt on my sleeve. I learned that not everyone was my friend or support system. I had to use wisdom and discernment when I built relationships with people and only associate with those who love and support me unconditionally and vice versa.

If I did not check my emotions at the door, I would end up in a mental institution, and if that happened, there would be no one to care for my children who desperately need me.

I also learned that if I wanted to succeed financially, I had to understand my emotions and where they came from. So much of what we do with our money is based on our emotions. We try to buy friendships, happiness, and love. We make huge mistakes financially based on our emotions, which can often lead to debt and bankruptcy.

Once I learned how to control my emotions, I was able to build my net worth, my credit score, and my bank account. I was able to get the life of abundance that I had envisioned for myself and my children.

I share this story because it was a pivotal point for me to understand that it is important to keep your emotions in check so that they don't go crazy, and no results are achieved. This chapter will help you control your emotions so you can achieve a beautiful abundant life without negativity getting in the way.

We'll be discussing a few points:

- Why humans are emotional creatures.
- Why your emotions are important.
- How to control your emotions.
- Ways to keep your emotions in check so you can get the life you've been waiting for.

By the end of the chapter, you will know how to control what you're feeling so that it no longer affects your mindset or the decisions that you make.

Humans Are Emotional Creatures

Human beings are emotional creatures by nature; that is the way God designed us. First, he gave us seven senses to navigate the world we live in. According to Pathways.org, those Seven Senses are:

- sight (Vision)

- hearing (Auditory)

- smell (Olfactory)

- taste (Gustatory)

- touch (Tactile)

- feel

- vestibular (Movement): the movement and balance sense, which gives us information about where our head and body are in space.

God gave us these seven senses because He wants us to have as human of an experience as possible. He wants to experience emotion and physical touch and sight. The human experience started when God created Adam and Eve in Genesis. He gave them the seven senses to do what they like with them; to have a full human experience. But instead, they disobeyed God and used their senses to fulfill their own pleasures, thus committing sin and being condemned to eternal torment.

God didn't give us these senses to merely sin. He gave them to us so we can enjoy and be fruitful. So, we can have a full human experience just as He offered Adam and Eve.

He also designed us with twenty-five distinct categories of emotions which encompass our body, mind, and spirit. According to Alan Cowen (2018), those twenty-five categories are:

- admiration

- adoration

- appreciation of beauty

- amusement

- anger

- anxiety

- awe

- awkwardness

- boredom

- calmness

- confusion

- craving

- disgust

- empathic pain

- entrancement

- excitement

- Fear

- horror

- interest

- joy

- nostalgia

- relief

- sadness

- satisfaction

- surprise

These emotions allow us to experience human life, even though we are made up of the soul that God entrusted our physical body with. Without these emotions, we'd act like robots, never really experiencing peace, joy, fulfillment, or even resilience and perseverance.

Why Are Emotions Important?

Emotions are important for various reasons, including:

- **They can motivate you in ways you never thought possible.** When you meet the person that you are meant to be with, The One, you experience a variety of emotions. Love, anxiety, excitement, curiosity—all these emotions can motivate you to act on them before it's too late. They help you understand what you need to do to act accordingly.

- **They can keep you safe.** When you are faced with a situation where your safety is in question, your emotions can literally save your life. They can help guide you to safety so that you are no longer in the danger zone.

- **They can encourage decision-making.** Although this can appear motivating, I want to put out a disclaimer. Even though listening to your emotions can help you decide on the best course for your life, sometimes this may not be a good thing. For example, what if you're trying to save money to go on vacation, and the shoes you've been eyeing finally go on sale? The excitement of your emotions may counteract your commitment to save money. Instead, your emotions motivate you to purchase the shoes, and now it's less money than you have in your savings account. I encourage you to keep this in mind when it comes to making decisions. Are your emotions steering you in the right direction? Or are they throwing you off course?

- **They can help with communication.** When you want to communicate with your partner about how you're feeling, you can use your emotions to help you navigate the conversation. This will make for a smoother conversation where you use your emotions to express how you feel.

Controlling Your Emotions

There are six basic emotions that we need to learn how to control. These emotions build the foundation for other sub-emotions to come into play.

- anger
- disgust
- fear
- happiness
- sadness
- surprise

According to the Bible, the one emotion that we need to learn how to control is anger: "Do not be quickly provoked in your spirit, for anger resides in the lap of fools" (*NIV*, 2011/1973, Ecclesiastes 7:9).

I recommend you read the entire chapter of Ecclesiastes 7 and the book of Proverbs. These books discuss wisdom and will assist you in how you should conduct your life.

Here's the thing I want you to remember: When you cannot control your emotions, it can lead to dire consequences physically, financially, and emotionally. People who do not control their emotions can end up with their freedom taken from them. It can cause potential disarray in your life and lead you down a path that brings you closer to Satan. I know, as a believer, this is not what you want. You want to get closer to God and live the life He has designed for you—controlling your emotions is a big step in that direction.

How you express yourself or deal with people can make the difference between life and death.

As instructed in I Thessalonians 4, "Each of you should learn to control your own body in a way that is holy and honorable" (*NIV*, 2011/1973, 4:4).

There are times when anger is necessary, but we need to determine when that is. The only way to really determine when and how you should use your anger wisely is through prayer.

To encourage you, this is what the bible says: "Do not be anxious about anything, but in everything by prayer and supplication with thanksgiving let your requests be made known to God. And the peace of God, which surpasses all understanding, will guard your hearts and your minds in Christ Jesus" (*NIV*, 2011/1973, Philippians 4: 6-7).

As I shared in my story at the beginning of this chapter, if I didn't learn to control my emotions, especially anger, I would experience a life of torment, regret, frustration, and all the other negative emotions you want to add. I would've for sure ended up in a mental institution knowing how bitter I felt I knew my kids deserved better than that. They deserved better from me.

Getting Your Emotions, Getting Your Life

Nowadays there are so many resources available for mental health. It no longer holds the stigma it used to, which is a phenomenal thing! In my culture, as an Afro-Cuban woman, the way we dealt with mental health issues was via the kitchen table and through Jesus and prayer. And sometimes, if it came down to it, we would give someone a good old fashion East Coast cussing out!

You could sit around the kitchen table with your close family members and discuss your issues, which sometimes helped, but most of the time, you were told that you don't have time to be crazy; crazy is reserved for white folks! You have kids to take care of and a husband to care for— why are you mad?!

Another thing we were also told was that we did not need counseling; all we needed was Jesus. And sometimes, we needed both to help us through.

I am so grateful we have evolved, and times are not like how it used to be. Thank you, God! Mental health services are no longer reserved for the rich and white folk. There are now services designed for people of color and every spiritual persuasion.

So how can you get your emotions so you can get your life?

Here are a few suggestions:

Be Positive

Research shows that how you think about yourself can have a powerful effect on how you feel. When we perceive ourselves and our life negatively, we can end up viewing experiences in a way that confirms that notion. I always say that when you focus on the positive aspects of life, you bring more positive results.

It's very similar to *The Secret,* by Rhonda Byrne: like attracts like. When you are positive, you attract more positivity into your life. When you're negative, you trigger a ripple effect of negativity. If you want to truly get your life so you can live it abundantly, find a way to be positive.

Be Grateful

Gratitude has been clearly linked with improved well-being and mental health as well as happiness. I call this counting your blessings and naming them one by one. If you have a roof over your head, clothes on your back, and food in your cupboards, while also being in reasonably good health, you are blessed.

Very similar to the "like attracts like" scenario, when you are grateful for all that you have, you will receive more things to be grateful for. Thank God for all those things. One effective way to envision gratefulness is to spend some time writing in a gratitude journal. Write down all the things you're grateful for so you can see them on paper as clearly as day. That way, you know and remember everything that is currently a part of your life that you can express gratitude for.

Focus on One Thing

Being mindful of the present moment allows us to let go of negative or difficult emotions from past moments or experiences that are weighing us down. When negative emotions arise, and they will, I like to clean my house or write in my journal. Cleaning allows you to work out physically and helps calm your mind and bring it into a peaceful state. Keeping a journal literally saved my life! Journaling allows you to put those emotions on paper so you can release them and focus on the plans that God has for you. When I was going through my darkest times, my journal was my lifeline.

Find a Friend

No man/woman is an island. I encourage you not to isolate yourself, especially when you are facing challenging times. You can join a church to help create a sense of community around you. However, if that is not your thing, find a social or charitable group and volunteer with organizations that you have a passion for. Find opportunities to meet people. It is important because these opportunities are great reminders that you are not alone in this journey and that many of us are going through emotional turmoil. It is important we stick together.

Do Something for Someone Else

The meaning you find in helping others will enrich and expand your life. –Dr. Patricia Harteneck

Research shows that being helpful and giving back to others has a beneficial effect on how you feel about yourself. Being helpful, kind, and valued for what you do is a wonderful way to build self-esteem.

Take a Break

In those moments when it all just seems like too much, I encourage you to step away for a moment. I believe in vacations—short, long, a couple of days—the timeframe doesn't matter. When things get extremely stressful, jump on a plane. If this is not feasible now, take a drive. Go away for a couple of days. Invest in a staycation. The point is to take a breather.

At one point in my life, I was traveling somewhere every three months. It allowed me to break unhealthy habits, gain perspective in a unique environment, and help me see my situation more clearly. If you cannot afford to travel on a plane, take a few days and go camping or stay in a nearby town. Set up a spa day for yourself or lounge in the backyard by the pool if you have one. Read an enjoyable book. Just take time for yourself. We'll speak more about the importance of self-care in Chapter Seven.

Start Today

Do not wait until you are in crisis. You have the power to take positive steps to improve your emotional health. Despite what people may say, self-care is not selfish. It is the least selfish thing you can do.

Here's how you can start:

- **Pray:** Ask God to show you the areas you need to improve on.

- **Act:** Faith without works is dead (James 2:26). Every response comes with a correlating action.

- **Wait:** Do not give up, wait on the Lord, and He will strengthen your heart. Wait, I say, on the Lord! "But those who hope in the Lord will renew their strength. They will soar on wings like eagles; they will run and not grow weary, they will walk and not be faint" (*NIV*, 2011/1973, Isaiah 40:31).

Meditation

Here are a few bible verses that I'd like to offer you to meditate on. Reading up on them and relating them to your life and your current situation will help you control and manage your emotions a bit better.

- Ephesians 4:31

- Matthew 19:20-22

- Ecclesiastes 11:10

- Philippians 2:13-15

- Romans 2:5-6

- Deuteronomy 31:8

- Philippians 4:8

- James 4:11

- Luke 12:15

- Proverbs 11:2

As you can attest from this chapter, controlling our emotions is vitally important to living an abundant life. When we are always experiencing negative emotions, how is it even possible to go after any type of abundance? It becomes difficult and rather overwhelming. Going through this chapter helped you understand that if you want to get your life, you need to get your emotions too! They both go hand in hand.

Some of the key points I'd like you to remember from this chapter are:

- When you experience negativity, you receive more negativity. Focus on positivity and watch your life shift for the better.

- Start today and do not wait. I encourage you to wait on the Lord, but if you want to truly transform your life, start acting on the things you need to do.

- Gratitude can set you up for incredible success. Keep a gratitude journal and write in it consistently so you can become a walking testimony of blessings for others.

- It is important to give back and help others. Use the time you have on this Earth to find ways to serve your community.

- Be mindful. Focus on the present moment and release all distractions from your life.

- It's okay to take breaks when you're struggling. Go for a walk, take a staycation, or jump on a plane and let your heart lead you to where you want to go. The point is to relax so you can get back to your daily activities with a clear and grateful mindset.

In Chapter 6, we'll be discussing ways to release your poverty mindset so you can shift into an abundance mindset. I also share a powerful testimony of how God took me out of scarcity and helped me become a multi-millionaire!

The vision that God gave you… it is meant for you. Chapter 6 will show you how you can achieve it.

Chapter 6:

Rags to Riches: Releasing the Poverty Mindset

Growing up, as I stated in Chapter 2, my family lived on welfare for all my childhood years. That means from birth until I was 18 years old, we collected welfare checks. I grew up in the inner city of Boston, living in poverty. How did I go from having a net worth of zero, living on welfare checks, to having a net worth of 1.5 million dollars?

The simple answer: Vision.

The more complicated answer: Strategy.

I always envisioned myself helping people in some form or another. I could not reconcile in my mind that all the unfortunate things that happened to me in my life were for nothing. There had to be a purpose for my life, and to fulfill that purpose, living in poverty and with a scarcity mindset was not an option.

There was no way I could be a blessing to others if I was completely disheveled mentally, spiritually, and financially. I needed to shift my mindset and come back to God so I can feel fulfilled in every area of my life. Once I experienced fulfillment, I could use what I learned in my own journey to be a blessing to others. To help them shift their story just as I had worked to shift mine. But I needed to work on myself first. Then the rest would follow.

In this chapter, I'll be speaking about the importance of creating both a vision and a strategy to achieve financial prosperity. Many people believe they can do one without the other, and for a season they can, but eventually, they'll lose sight of their goals. When you have a strong vision, creating a strategy to achieve that vision will feel easier. Your vision will keep you going. When you have the right strategies in place, they will work as long as you remain focused on the vision of why you're following the strategies in the first place. See, they both go hand in hand. In the long term, one cannot work without the other.

We'll also be addressing the following points:

- God's promises for your life.

- Envisioning what God is calling you to do.

- The importance of wisdom and how it applies to your life.

- The importance of educating yourself regarding your finances.

- How to empower yourself to get out of debt so you don't experience financial burden.

- The importance of establishing an excellent credit score and what you can do so it stays in good standing.

- The best investment you can make for your long-term goals.

- Ways to save money.

- Understanding the difference between assets and liabilities.

- Understanding your net worth.

This chapter will introduce a variety of different things to help you begin thinking about your long-term goals and achievements. By the end of this chapter, you should be able to gather a better idea of how to strategize and create a remarkable vision for your life so you can continue embracing an abundant and prosperous mindset.

Envision the Future

For you to envision your future, you need to know what your vision is. It sounds cliche, but it's the truth. If you don't know what your vision is or what it stands for—or even what it means to have a vision—then how can you envision your future? It's as if you're hitting a wall that never breaks or throwing spaghetti to the wall, never knowing if it will stick.

By meditating on God's word, your vision will be revealed, and you'll receive clarity and confirmation. Proverbs 29 says, "Where there is no vision, the people perish" (*KJV*, 2021/1611, Proverbs 29:18). In other words, if you don't have a vision for where you want your life to go, you'll always feel lost, confused, and overwhelmed.

Before we move further into the topic of vision, it is important to understand what the technical definition of vision is so you can have a deeper understanding. According to the Oxford Dictionary, vision is "the faculty or state of being able to see; or the ability to think about or plan the future with imagination or wisdom" (n.d.).

Now what is God's definition of vision? He calls it a *prophecy* in Joel 2:28 and a *revelation* in Habakkuk 2:2. And Numbers 12, He speaks of vision as a revelation to a prophet in the form of dreams.

These verses demonstrate that by meditating on God's word, He will reveal the vision He has for your life with clarity. He will speak to you through people close to you and even, perhaps, through members of the congregation. When you understand His messages for your life, it is your job to listen, obey, and act on the vision.

Now, when it comes to the Oxford Dictionary's definition of vision, it shows that your imagination will never steer you wrong and that it is important to keep dreaming and keep visualizing your future. Your vision may not be clear to others, but that's okay. This is why it's your vision and not theirs—keep going with it and keep moving toward it.

How Do You Get a Vision?

To receive God's vision for your life, I encourage you to pray. Pray for your purpose and pray for God to reveal the visions and dreams He has for you. They're all a part of an everlasting life with Him in His kingdom.

If you wish, you can use this prayer or you can create your own:

Lord God, thank you for allowing me to dream. You have given me a purpose in this life, so I praise you and I am thankful to you for guiding me toward it and showing me the next steps. Ephesians 1:11 reveals that I have been chosen according to your perfect plan and that you align everything according to your will. I pray for utmost certainty. I pray for your guiding light to shine on my vision and my purpose. Give me clarity on what you want me to do. I will listen and I will obey. Speak through my heart so I may hear your revelation and I may gain wisdom to fulfill the duties you ask of me. Grant me peace through this journey and light my path. I pray that You make my path straight (Proverbs 3:6) so I know that this vision comes from You. I promise to cherish this vision and I promise to honor it for all eternity so that it may be fulfilled with your Holy Spirit guiding my inner being. In Jesus's name, I pray. Amen.

Instead of looking at your current circumstance, as most of us tend to do because it's comfortable, envision where God would want you to be. There are many examples of people who grew up in extreme poverty and who are now wealthy. You don't even have to go far. I am sure there are people in your world right now who have come a long way financially. They received their breakthrough—now it's your turn. You are no different from these people. They pee and bleed just like you. They put their shoes on just like you. They put their pants on one leg at a time. God can reveal a vision to you far greater than you can even comprehend right now, but you need to be ready to hear it. You need to be ready for the vision that He has for your life so you can fulfill it in His honor. For the glory of His kingdom. He reveals it to you and you alone because it is *for* you. You are the only one that can succeed in this purpose. This is the most amazing thing about revelations and prophecies.

But here's the thing. A disclaimer if you will. While it is your job to fulfill God's vision for you on this earth, it is Satan's job to do whatever he can to destroy you and deter you from fulfilling your purpose. He'll instill fears and insecurities so that you lose your confidence and believe that this purpose is not meant for you. If you begin to feel this way, please remind yourself of Chapter Four—Free Your Mind, The Rest Will Follow. If you need a refresher, consider this God's revelation for you to read it again. Seek prayer, wisdom, and comfort from the Lord to know when the enemy is trying to steer you off course from walking the light-filled path as you venture toward your vision and purpose.

Using Your Imagination

Now to him who is able to do immeasurably more than all we ask or imagine, according to his power that is at work within us, to him be glory in the church and in Christ Jesus throughout all generations, for ever and ever! Amen. –Ephesians 3:20

Many times, we have a strong vision for how we want our life to be but let me be clear—this vision is not because we thought of it ourselves; it showed up in our minds because it is a vision that God has for our life. He can speak to us through dreams, passages we read in the Bible, through other people, or even through messages we read on social media.

Now, using our imagination allows us to be creative and helps enhance that vision. God wants us to use our imagination as much as possible. He wants us to develop our creativity and live the most abundant life we can achieve.

Now, the question boils down to this: How does God want us to use our imagination so that we live a fulfilling, abundant life? There are three possible scenarios that I would like to share with you below.

Use Your Imagination to Remember His Promises

God has given us so many promises for a greater life. We can use our imagination to not only remember them, but to imagine those promises being fulfilled.

There are over 3,500 promises in the Bible that God has given us (Core Radiate, 2018). Now, imagine you are fulfilling each one. Remember John 3:16? "For God so loved the world that He gave His only begotten Son, that whosoever believes in Him should not perish but have everlasting life" (*KJV*, 2021/1611). It is in this verse that God promises an abundant life, so long as you are a Believer. Now, imagine how this verse applies to your life. Imagine His promises coming to fruition. Would you feel hope? Peace? Joy? Excitement? Love? Supported? I trust that if you picture this verse in your mind and meditate on it every time you are facing a challenge, God will bring peace into your spirit and a wave of calm into your life.

God's infinite promise in the book of Jeremiah is also very similar— "For I know the plans I have for you," declares the LORD, "plans to prosper you and not to harm you, plans to give you hope and a future" (*NIV*, 2011/1973, Jeremiah 29:11). His promise for an abundant life is right there in these words. Imagine this promise in your heart when you find yourself questioning whether you're on the right path or not. Imagining these words can give you comfort in times of stress and when things don't feel like they're working.

When you feel fear, imagining God's words from Isaiah 41:10 and Deuteronomy 31:8 will help bring you peace and comfort, knowing that

God is always by your side, guiding you, and bringing you hope even in your darkest hour.

There are so many other biblical promises that can offer us a greater life when we imagine them being fulfilled. God never wavers; nor does he offer empty, broken promises. When He says he'll lead us to the light when we are surrounded by darkness (*NIV*, 2011/1973, Ephesians 5:11-14), you can be sure that promise will be fulfilled.

Use Your Imagination to Understand God's Purpose for Your Life

We are all given a purpose that God wants us to fulfill during our time in this world. Using our imagination to see that purpose first, before it comes to fruition, allows us to fully trust God and have faith knowing that it will be fulfilled in a remarkable way.

Jesus sees potential in all of us. We may not see it in ourselves at that very moment, but the most important thing to do is to first trust God. Matthew 4:19 says, "Come, follow me" (*NIV*, 2011/1973). In this story, we learn about when Jesus first gathered His disciples. The soon-to-be disciples were merely fishermen, but Jesus saw potential in them to be part of His team. To them, they were only fishermen, trying to make a living and eat, but God saw them with a stronger purpose. When He called them to follow Him, they did not question but trusted Him and became obedient. They left things just as they were, not knowing what was going to happen, and they followed just as they were instructed to do.

As we think about this story, something profound is revealed. At the moment, we may not know what God's purpose for our lives is, but in due time, He will show us. He will reveal what our next steps are and what we are required to do–the challenge is to listen and be obedient. As humans, we may think, "I can't do that" or "That's impossible," but it's important to remember that if we are being called to achieve our God-given purpose, it's because God noticed our potential before we can even comprehend it. He noticed that we are fully capable, and we can withstand any challenges that relate to our purpose and so it is important to trust Him and follow His guidance.

In Matthew 4, Peter and the other disciples were fishermen; they may have thought that this duty was the only thing they were capable of doing. But God thought otherwise. He saw their potential to strengthen and grow the church as disciples of the Most High, so He called on them. And without hesitation, they followed His leadership and did something extraordinary as Jesus' right hand.

When understanding your purpose, imagine how God can use your gifts and your unique capabilities to bless others. Be open to what God is calling you to do, without question. Imagine the joy it can bring to God's kingdom when you fulfill your purpose by simply being obedient and faithful to God's call: "Live a life worthy of the calling you have received" (*NIV*, 2011/1973, Ephesians 4:1).

Use Your Imagination to Be Reminded of His Blessings

Every single day, we are surrounded by God's blessings. We are surrounded by His abundance, and we are constantly being guided by His spirit. When we imagine what He has done for us—the tribulations He's helped us overcome, how He has watched over us and taken care of our friends and family, the danger He's pulled us through—we can be in awe of His grace and splendor.

There have been many times where we've felt like, "I have no idea how I was able to overcome that situation, it must be God;" and sure enough, it has been. There are situations where it feels too big. It feels as though it's too difficult to even fathom or comprehend—in these instances, it is important to imagine His blessings pouring out into your life. Healing you, strengthening you, comforting you–giving you peace. God's word in John 16 says it all: "I have overcome the world" (*NIV*, 2011/1973, John 16:33).

When you're experiencing trials, imagine God's spirit transforming you from the inside out. Imagine His healing power rejuvenating you and His purpose is revealed to you. Imagine yourself trusting Him completely because He has already won your battles. Remind yourself that His grace and tender spirit dwells in you (1 Corinthians 3:16) and because of this, you are sons and daughters of the Most High King.

When God Gives You Your Vision

Throughout our entire life, God gives us many visions. They could be a vision for our career or business, relationships, family, or even for our church. And just as I've been emphasizing throughout this chapter, when God gives us a vision, it is important to listen and obey. He visualizes a beautiful and prosperous life for us so when He sets a vision on our heart, we need to listen and honor it and take the next steps toward the vision when asked to do so.

With this being said, there are four ways that God shows us how He wants us to work toward our vision.

Unshakeable Desire

When our vision is strong and clear enough, God will show us that we have an unshakeable desire to pursue what He wants us to do. It doesn't matter how many challenges we experience or whether it feels like things are not working—our unshakeable desire gives us the strength to push forward. This desire moves us to action when we don't feel motivated, and it pushes us past our limits.

But here's something that we need to remember—it is not by our strength that we continue to move forward when times are rough; rather, it is by the infinite and spiritual strength within us that God gives us. It's this strength that reminds us to keep going and to remember our vision. It's this strength that builds our unshakeable desire to accomplish our goals. It's not because we're pretty; it's because we believe in the power of Jesus Christ that works through us and among us every single day of our lives.

Doors Will Open to Unexpected Opportunities

Just as God will give us an unshakeable desire to commit to achieving our goals, He will also not only close doors that are not a part of our vision, but He will open doors that we didn't expect to be open.

God's word says in Colossians 4 to "make the most out of every opportunity."

> And pray for us, too, that God may open a door for our message, so that we may proclaim the mystery of Christ, for which I am in chains. Pray that I may proclaim it clearly, as I should. Be wise in the way you act toward outsiders; make the most of every opportunity. (*NIV*, 2011/1973, Colossians 4:3-5)

When we have a strong vision, we need God to open doors so this vision can become a reality. At times, these doors would open when we least expected them. We may expect one door to open because we feel it's the "right one to make things happen," but God will close that one and open a completely different door—one that may astound us and make us question why it's opening because we never prayed for it.

But that's the thing about a God-given vision. God will generally not open doors that we pray hard to open; He will open doors that are unexpected yet are a *huge* step toward fulfilling our vision. The trick is to not question why it's opening but to just go with it. Just as I said when I shared the story about the disciples earlier: Peter, Andrew, James, and John were simply fishing, but Jesus called on them to follow Him so they can fulfill a greater purpose. He opened that door to their calling, and without question, they walked through. If a door is opening that leads to an unexpected circumstance, I encourage you to trust it. Rather than question it, fulfill the plan. God is opening that door; walk through with confidence.

Bible Verses Will Show Us the Next Steps

Once we have the unshakeable desire to fulfill our goals and God is opening doors, we must seek the words of Jesus Christ. By studying the bible and meditating on the verses that apply to our vision, God will show us the next steps.

Having an open mind and listening to what God has to say can greatly lead us in the right direction. We may not know the next steps and we may question when God opens doors, especially ones that we least expect, but meditating on the Scriptures can help give us the clarity that we need.

In Psalms, it says, "Your word is a lamp to my feet and a light to my path" (*NIV*, 2011/1973, Psalms 119:105). When God gives us a word that helps direct our path, it can only be of encouragement and hope. It can be a message of trust, motivation, and inspiration. *A light to my path...* God directs us through the Scriptures, even though it may not feel that way at times. By reading the Scriptures, God gives you the wisdom to succeed in your vision and shows you how to apply the verse in your life so that your vision becomes stronger. You no longer question your vision; you simply trust the Spirit that things are working, and the Scriptures serve as a reminder that they are.

God Will Guide Us Through the Sacrifices

For us to go after our vision with everything we have, there are going to be sacrifices–things that we'll need to give up to live a better life. They could be toxic friends or environments, health concerns such as smoking or drinking, a toxic relationship with our spouse, a job, or an opportunity. Most of these things are usually dear to us, such as the relationship with our best friend or partner, but the way I see it, if God is asking us to give them up and let them go, it's because He is helping you make room for brighter, positive things.

Just as it says in Romans 12, "present your bodies as a living sacrifice" *(NIV, 2011/1973, Romans 12:1-2)*. Of course, this statement is not literal, but it demonstrates that God is asking you to give your all to Him so you can achieve an abundant life, even if that means letting go of things that don't serve you or God's vision for your life.

Strategize to Become Better

Now that we've discussed how to envision the future using God's will for our life, we can talk about the next piece: strategy and wisdom.

How do you get from point A to point B where money is concerned? Get ready for a journey as I take you down the "Yellow Brick Road."

After two divorces I experienced, I became bankrupt. My ex-husbands were supposed to provide child support and alimony, but that never happened. Neither one did. Of course, my credit was very low and because of this, I experienced foreclosure on my home, and I became homeless. Back on welfare, I went. I had three small children to raise so food stamps and regular county checks were necessary. I had to swallow my pride.

One of the first things I realized was that being on welfare with an education was an incredible advantage. I was already ahead of the game compared to my counterparts who were uneducated. I had acquired many skills that allowed me to market them, and if I didn't have a particular set of skills, I would go back to school and acquire them. I did what most people struggle with—I became resourceful.

Just as Isaiah 40:31 states, "But those who hope in the Lord will renew their strength. They will soar on wings like eagles; they will run and not grow weary, they will walk and not be faint (*NIV*, 2011/1973).

I believed God would take me and my children out of the mess we were in as long as I continued to have faith and become resourceful with what I had. I acquired skills that helped me survive and keep my children safe—it didn't matter if I was on welfare or used food stamps— resourcefulness helped me take care of my children and helped God take care of me.

It's great to have a vision, but if we don't plan and strategize to help our vision come to fruition, our vision becomes pointless. Becoming resourceful as we take steps toward our vision is part of that strategy. There are so many things we can offer ourselves and the world; God told us not to be weary, but to have faith and hope so our strength can be renewed. By identifying the strategies, we need to put in place, our vision will feel one step closer.

The Importance of Wisdom

The beginning of wisdom is this: Get wisdom. Though it costs all you have, get an understanding. –Proverbs 4:7

In many of the verses in Proverbs, wisdom is described as a form of wealth. "For wisdom is better than rubies, and all the things one may desire cannot be compared with her" (*NIV*, 2011/1973, Proverbs 8:11) and "How much better to get wisdom than gold!" (*NIV*, 2011/1973, Proverbs 16:16).

Contrary to secular belief, God's Word states that it is better to acquire wisdom than to accumulate monetary riches, for wisdom can also make you wealthy. Many materialistic people who believe that being financially rich is the greatest thing in the world may disagree with this statement. However, believers take this statement to heart.

Think about it. When we are struggling, what do we usually do? We turn to the Bible. We read God's Word. We seek wisdom to renew our strength. We don't go to the mall and purchase something, thinking it will make us feel better; we increase our wisdom by strengthening our relationship with the Lord. We continue to seek wisdom until we find what we are looking for and until our hope is restored. This is how we believers think and how we strategize. We strategize with the Lord by seeking His wisdom, and His grace shows us what to do.

We Can't Work on Knowledge Alone

Many may think that knowledge and wisdom are the same, but they are, indeed, different. Wisdom is the discernment to know right from wrong, and knowledge is the first step in acquiring wisdom.

For example, if you desire to work out, you can gain all the knowledge you want to become healthier. You can research recipes, the right workouts for your body type, and the daily activities you can do to energize and tone. However, to put all the knowledge you've learned to the test, you include wisdom to know what is right for your body or not. For instance, wisdom tells you that fruits and vegetables are excellent nourishment to keep you healthy, but eating chips or drinking pop is not. If you have a bad back, wisdom tells you that traditional sit-ups won't be a good idea, but perhaps you can engage in a modified version.

Based on this example, knowledge alone cannot be a strategy. We must utilize the wisdom we have obtained because of this knowledge, as both go hand in hand in figuring out the next steps for our life.

Proverbs 4:11-12 teaches that wisdom helps us learn the difference between right and wrong. Wisdom helps us understand the implications of the choices we make. If we're upset about something, wisdom helps us understand why.

What Is Wisdom?

One's philosophy is not expressed in words; it is expressed in the choices we make... and the choices we make are ultimately our responsibility. –Eleanor Roosevelt

According to BetterHelp, wisdom "requires a deep level of thinking" (2022). Now, when we think about this in the spiritual sense, God gives us wisdom to help us think through our decisions. Especially when we experience difficult situations that we are not sure how to overcome, we seek God to give us the wisdom we need to push through these barriers and come out on the other side full of hope. God helps us overcome them because of the wisdom we asked for.

Let's say you're stressed because you're not sure how to complete a project. You can seek God and ask Him to give you the clarity you need to move forward successfully. This clarity gives you the wisdom to understand what the next step is, and once you've completed that step, you receive more wisdom to surpass the next challenge.

All this falls in line with what God is asking you to do. When you're unsure of what to do next so you can move closer to your vision, I encourage you to pray to God. Ask Him to give you wisdom and discernment to understand the next step. Ask Him for wisdom so you can break free of limitations, doubt, and judgment. Ask Him to help you see clearly so you're no longer doubting yourself but instead, you acquire the wisdom and knowledge you need to step forward with confidence.

Bible Verses on Wisdom

Many bible verses help explain wisdom. Here are a few to meditate on when you are looking for guidance from the Lord:

- "Trust in the Lord with all your heart and lean not on your own understanding; in all your ways submit to him, and he will make your paths straight" (*NIV*, 2011/1973, Proverbs 3:5-6).

- "If any of you lacks wisdom, you should ask God, who gives generously to all without finding fault, and it will be given to you" (*NIV*, 2011/1973, James 1:5).

- "Wisdom is a shelter as money is a shelter, but the advantage of knowledge is this: Wisdom preserves those who have it" (*NIV*, 2011/1973, Ecclesiastes 7:12).

- "Who is like the wise? Who knows the explanation of things? A person's wisdom brightens their face and changes its hard appearance" (*NIV*, 2011/1973, Ecclesiastes 8:1).

- "Blessed are those who find wisdom, those who gain understanding" (*NIV*, 2011/1973, Proverbs 3:13).

- "Her ways are pleasant ways, and all her paths are peace. She is a tree of life to those who take hold of her; those who hold her fast will be blessed" (*NIV*, 2011/1973, Proverbs 3:17-18).

- "Therefore, everyone who hears these words of mine and puts them into practice is like a wise man who built his house on the rock" (*NIV*, 2011/1973, Matthew 7:24).

Wisdom Helps Us Grow

No matter what, we cannot do everything ourselves. It's impossible. As a popular saying goes, "It takes a village." When we try to do everything ourselves, a couple of things can happen:

- We get burned out, anxious, and overwhelmed.

- We'll want to call it quits.

- We can make ourselves physically sick due to exhaustion.

Although we acquire a ton of knowledge every single day, it means nothing unless we have the wisdom to think things through.

Sandra Carey says, "Never mistake knowledge for wisdom. One helps you make a living; the other helps you make a life" (n.d.). This means that with knowledge, you can create a career or business using the skills and expertise you've acquired, but when you have wisdom, it will help you grow and create the life of your dreams rather than simply survive.

Wisdom helps you become a greater version of yourself every single day. It helps you learn from your mistakes and failures and make better decisions today that will positively reflect on your life tomorrow. As I stated earlier, it's great to have knowledge, but wisdom will take you further in life than you ever thought possible. It teaches you grit, endurance, and stamina. It helps you take the higher road rather than be petty and prideful. Wisdom helps you grow and live even though you may feel you don't have enough knowledge to survive. Wisdom gives you the discernment to move forward, despite any challenges or obstacles you experience.

Educate Yourself Constantly

Educating yourself is key. Learn all you can about finances. Become financially literate. Please note that if you are receiving public assistance, there is no shame in that. The only shame that shows up is when you choose to stay on public assistance, and you feel there is no other option. There are always other options. God always blesses us with abundance and prosperity every single day—we simply need to be open to the offering.

There are several programs for a person to get a high school diploma, a college education, and vocational training.

Understanding Financial Literacy

During high school and college, we are taught about financial literacy. This entails understanding numbers, as well as how to budget and organize our finances. Throughout the many years we take accounting and all the other math classes in school, we acquire so much knowledge about finances and how to use it appropriately to live an abundant life.

In Chapter Seven, we'll be talking about the importance of having a beautiful relationship with money that requires financial literacy and that guides us on our journey to becoming financially abundant.

However, as we've discussed throughout this chapter, knowledge is simply not enough. You can gain as much knowledge as you'd like on how to organize your finances, but wisdom needs to be integrated so you know how to organize it appropriately.

Get Out of Debt

Let no debt remain outstanding, except the continuing debt to love one another, for whoever loves others has fulfilled the law. –NIV, 2011/1973, Romans 13:8

Filing for bankruptcy paid off my outstanding debts. I learned to live on cash only for several years until my credit report became clear. Thus, approximately seven years later, the bankruptcy came off my credit report, and I was free to start over.

I encourage you to watch your Debt Ratio. The Debt Ratio is the amount of debt you can comfortably handle after regular expenses— rent, mortgage, food, electricity, gas, and car payments if you have a car. That ratio is 30 percent of your total income. This means that if you go over the percentage, you will overextend yourself and find it hard to pay your bills, thus having to file for bankruptcy later because you've accumulated too much debt.

Establish Credit

The key to establishing good credit is to remember Proverbs 22:7: "The rich rule over the poor, and the borrower is the slave of the lender" (*NIV*, 2011/1973).

Watch your credit usage. It is not monopoly money. Pay your credit card off every month so you don't accumulate debt. At the very least, pay the minimum balance and do not be late with your payments. Creditors look at how responsible you are with your credit cards and the money you borrow, which determines how your credit score will be affected.

Here are a few tips to help you manage and maintain your credit, so it remains in good standing. If it currently is on the poor credit scale, these tips will help you get it back into good standing:

- Pay off the balance every month.

- Pay attention to what you're using your credit card for.

- Ensure you don't go over your balance and max out your credit.

- Save some money in your savings so it can act as a rainy-day fund in case you need to dip into it to pay off your credit card.

- Don't be late with payments. It usually becomes a ripple effect; when you're late one month, it can become a habit.

To give you an idea, here's a good rule of thumb with credit scores:

- **Poor:** 300-579

- **Fair:** 580-669

- **Good:** 670-739

- **Very good:** 740-799

- **Excellent:** 800-850

(Equifax, n.d.)

Buying Home & Land

Location, Location, Location. This is the key to purchasing property. Ideally, you want to purchase property in an area that will go up in value so you can get more bang for your buck when the real estate market is at its peak.

One good way to do this is to buy land. A lot of people do not think about land ownership, but owning a piece of land is ideal when building wealth.

Here are a few benefits that come with purchasing land:

- It's less work.

- It becomes residual income as you can lease out the land to prospective buyers, such as farmers.

- It can become a long-term investment that continues to accumulate income.

- It's less risky than owning physical property.

- It's more flexible. You can do whatever you'd like with your land in a way that produces the most income.

- Offers higher value down the road if you wish to sell it.

Why Real Estate Is the Best Investment

According to millionaires around the world, they go by their word: Real estate will always be the best investment you can make for your long-term goals.

Why do they say that? Here are a few reasons and then you can decide for yourself:

- It's long-term residual income. The income can continue for years and years to come.

- If you come across the right investment and you snatch it up right away, you can build excellent equity in your portfolio, especially if the property offers a ton of value and it's in an extraordinary location.

- Many people say that it is better to buy than rent. Rather than build equity for your landlord and continue to make money, why not start building equity for yourself and set your retirement up for success?

- There is unlimited potential. There are many real estate opportunities you can consider: Air BnB, foreclosures, condos, commercial, land, and vacation rentals.

- You'll always have buyers and renters. There will always be someone looking for a place to live—whether they purchase the property from you, and you use that money to buy another one, or they rent the property long-term, and you build an excellent relationship.

- You can use the money you receive from your property investments to invest in land and generate extra residual income.

Save Your Money

I cannot stress this enough: Save your money! It is important to create a savings account of six months to one year for expenses. By using this strategy, you'll never get into debt. Well, I shouldn't say *never...* you won't go into debt if you commit to this as a savings account for your expenses and you don't dip into it every chance you get.

I also encourage you to create a retirement account and an investment account. You can be set up for life if these accounts are in place. When it comes time to retire, you have your retirement account to fall back on, and you can dip into your investment account to purchase real estate to generate income while you're sipping margaritas on the beach during retirement.

It is also important to educate yourself on 401Ks, investments, and savings. It bears repeating that you need to increase your knowledge but also generate wisdom based on that knowledge to ensure success.

I've learned in my own journey that the key to saving money is to think long-term. Create long-term strategies that will help generate income for you and your family's future.

Assets Versus Liabilities

I've also learned that the key to wealth is to think about assets versus liabilities.

What are assets?

An asset is a resource with economic value that an individual, corporation, or country owns or controls with the expectation that it will provide a future benefit.

Assets can include:

- properties/Homes
- land
- artwork
- jewelry
- coins and heirlooms
- escrow in mortgages

In other words, an asset is anything that will appreciate in value long-term.

What are liabilities?

Liabilities are any debts you have. They can be:

- bank loans
- mortgages
- unpaid bills
- IOUs
- credit cards
- car loans

If you have promised to pay someone a sum of money soon and you haven't paid them yet, that is considered a liability.

When you want to save money, it is vitally important that you decrease your liabilities. When you do this, your assets go up, and your net worth also increases as a result.

How to Save Money

There are a variety of ways to save money. I can offer you a few that have helped me:

- Understand how much you spend.

- Keep track of your spending.

- Add money into your savings account regularly, even if it's a small amount. Every little bit counts.

- Minimize your spending habits. If you notice you eat out way too much, start cooking at home.

- Look into automatic payments. Are there some payments you can let go of to help reduce your spending?

- Make saving a goal. Do you want to go on a vacation? Buy another property or your first one? When you have a goal in mind, you'll commit to saving.

- Understand what your financial obligations are. Which ones are most important? Focus on those priorities and see if you can minimize the others.

- Keep accumulating your savings account. Start small and eventually, it will grow and abundantly increase.

Net Worth

You've heard me speak about net worth throughout this chapter. You may be new to the term so you may not have an idea of what it is. Here is a simple explanation:

Net worth is the total wealth of an individual, company, or household. It is determined by looking at all the individual's financial assets and liabilities.

So how can you calculate what your net worth is?

It's quite simple. Subtract your liabilities from your assets (Investopedia, 2023) and you have your net worth. You can have a positive net worth or a negative net worth. If you are in the positive, it's because you have accumulated more assets than liabilities. If you are in the negative, you have accumulated more debt than money-making activities. In other words, you spend way too much money; maybe even more money than you currently make.

To shift it around, find ways to decrease your liabilities, and eventually, your net worth will increase, and you'll become more financially valuable.

The Bible says,

> He will love you and bless you and increase your numbers. He will bless the fruit of your womb, the crops of your land—your grain, new wine, and olive oil—the calves of your herds and the lambs of your flocks in the land he swore to your ancestors to give you. (*NIV*, 2011/1973, Deuteronomy 7:13)

I am a living witness that this is true. The first thing in receiving true wealth is to believe that God wants to bless you, and you are worthy of receiving that blessing!

Use wisdom in handling all your financial matters. It is important that you do not squander your time or your money, as they are both valuable—indeed, they are what dreams are made of.

Meditation

Here are a few bible verses for you to reflect on for guidance when working on increasing your assets.

These passages have helped and encouraged me on my journey, so I know they can help you too:

- Proverbs 22:4
- Proverbs 9:10
- Proverbs 21:5
- Proverbs 10:22
- Psalm 127:2
- Proverbs 3:9-10
- Hebrews 13:5

I hope that this chapter has encouraged you to release the poverty mindset you may be holding onto. As you go through the remainder of the book, I encourage you to reflect on the verses that I have shared in this chapter; you can use them to affirm that you have a wealthy mindset every day.

In this chapter, we've learned many things:

- The difference between assets and liabilities.
- Ways to increase your net worth (decrease your liabilities so your assets can grow).
- The best investment move you can make for your long-term future.
- Ways to continually save money.
- Understanding why knowledge is not enough. You also need wisdom to help consolidate your success.

- The importance of using your imagination to enhance your God-given vision.

In the next chapter, we'll be discussing the importance of giving yourself time and space to establish and recognize your priorities. It will offer you some knowledge on how to develop extraordinary strategies, so you no longer feel overwhelmed when trying to achieve an abundant life. You're no longer trying, but you're succeeding, knowing God is on your side.

Chapter 7:

Money Answers All Things—How to Achieve Balance in Your Pursuit of the All-Mighty Dollar

If you are looking to obtain an abundant life, one that is prosperous and God-driven, your focus should not be purely on money. When pursuing your passion, whether it is a career, starting a business, or writing a great American novel, we know the money will come. In our current society, it is all about the hustle and chasing the checks—that is okay up to a point. In Ecclesiastes 10:19, the Bible says, "A feast is made for laughter, and wine maketh merry; but money answereth all things" (*KJV*, 2021/1611).

However, when you focus entirely on just making a profit or where the money is coming from, you can become desensitized to spiritual things and thrown off course away from Godly beliefs. Hence the importance of creating a balance between making money and living an abundant life with God.

When I first started out in my writing career, my focus was on the pure joy of writing. All I wanted was for my writing to help people—that was my hope. But, of course, there did come a time when I started to worry about how much money I was making as an author. To be honest, it almost caused me to quit writing. I started to distance myself from my true God-given purpose. I truly felt the struggle here.

But one day, God impressed upon my heart that writing was a gift from Him and Him alone and that if I stayed true to that gift, then the money would come. When thinking about this, the scripture that comes to mind is Psalms 45:1: "My heart is indicting a good matter: I speak of the things which I have made touching the king: my tongue is the pen of a ready writer" (*KJV, 2021/1611*).

I held on to my gift, and eventually, I became a New York Times bestselling author!

It is true—we cannot live without money. We need money to survive; that's a given. A smile may brighten a person's day and that is free, but if you see a hungry child or a homeless person on the street, a smile and prayers will not cut it. Unfortunately, they cannot survive on prayers alone.

In Proverbs 19:17, God's word says: "Whoever is kind to the poor lends to the LORD, and he will reward them for what they have done" (*NIV, 2011/1973*). Giving a smile, offering a prayer, and a few dollars to the homeless man constitutes kindness because the Lord loves a cheerful giver (2 Corinthians 9:7). Offering food to hungry children becomes a good deed in the eyes of Christ, and therefore, He will reward you handsomely in the future.

This chapter is about helping you create a perfect balance with God by your side in every moment. We'll learn about the importance of priorities, setting attainable goals, and having a healthy relationship with money. The relationship we currently have with money determines our abundance in the future. To do all of this, it is also important that you have a healthy relationship with yourself, and that starts with taking care of yourself mentally, emotionally, spiritually, and physically every single day.

This chapter will help you to put your best foot forward so that you may succeed in reaching abundance every day. God only wants good things for you; this chapter is a good demonstration of how He continues to guide you.

Establishing Priorities

One of the first things to do to create a harmonious balance in your life is to establish your priorities. Figure out what is most important for you and then hold your boundaries when it comes to it. Establishing priorities and establishing boundaries at the same time tends to be tricky. Deciding on your priorities can be easy, but when it comes to holding your boundaries, it can be a struggle.

As believers, it is in our nature to give and serve our community as much as we can. God's Word says, "And do not forget to do good and to share with others, for with such sacrifices God is pleased" (*NIV*, 2011/1973, Hebrews 13:16). While we are compassionate like that, it is very important to set some ground rules for ourselves and set priorities, so we're not pulled in every direction.

When establishing priorities, I encourage you to set aside some time to create your list. Think of it as a to-do list that helps hold you accountable for keeping up with your priorities.

For example, if you visualize yourself traveling the world and speaking about the love of Jesus at conferences and events, maybe one of your priorities could be to create or finish your website so that it's ready to go for when God shows you when and where your first trip will be. Of course, with anything we may do, it is important to pray about it and seek God's wisdom and guidance. As you pray, ask Him to help you acknowledge your priorities and establish them so that you have the discernment to hold yourself accountable for taking the steps you need to take.

Setting Your Priorities

Four ways will help you set priorities successfully:

- **A to-do list:** As already stated, creating a to-do list will help keep you organized and less overwhelmed. The items on your list can be either business-oriented or personal priorities if you wish. By writing them down, you can keep track of what you need to be doing that will bring you one step closer to the vision God has entrusted you with.

- **Rank the order of importance:** Now that you've created your list, you can go through each item and decide which are the top priorities to accomplish. Once you've established which holds the most priority, you can complete those items first, while holding off on the ones with the least priority. Ranking your list can help with organization as well as keeping you on track with the things you committed yourself to doing, rather than pushing them back.

- **Give yourself a time limit:** I'm not saying to compete with yourself, but allocating a specific amount of time to each item on your list will help you complete more tasks in less time. It will also help you minimize procrastination and distractions as you'll be solely focused on the tasks you need to complete.

- **Schedule your priorities in your calendar:** When they're in your calendar, they're confirmed. There is a certain satisfaction when you can cross off a task in your calendar. You feel accomplished. But visual people need to see a task in their calendar to be able to complete it; otherwise, if it's only a paper, they may forget, and it becomes neglected. If you're a visual person, adding your priorities to your calendar can keep you accountable for completing them that day, which brings you a step closer to your goals.

Creating Strategies for Your Priorities

Now that we've discussed how to set priorities, here are a few ways that will help you strategize when it comes to setting priorities.

Know When Everything Is Completed

Creating a to-do list is important to help keep you organized so you no longer feel overwhelmed. By keeping track of what you've done and crossing it off as it gets completed, you feel more accomplished and successful. You can breathe a bit more and be at peace. By crossing things off, you can focus on other priorities that require your attention and channel your productivity.

Release Attachment to the Outcome

It's great to have goals and vision, but it is important that you let go of your expectations. Let go and let God handle the results. God is always in control of your vision, so I encourage you to remind yourself that it's okay to let go of expectations. Just because something doesn't go the way you expected it to, it doesn't mean it's not for you. It simply means that God has a more extraordinary plan for you. I encourage you to be open to unexpected possibilities. Let go and let God.

Set Achievable Priorities

It is important to be realistic with your priorities. If your vision is to speak on stages around the world sharing the word of God, one of your priorities could be to book speaking gigs at your local church first. It feels achievable and a great step toward your overall vision. To break this down even further, maybe you can start sharing your message with your viewers by going on Facebook Live and using that as your preliminary stage. By setting realistic priorities, you're able to achieve them at a more efficient pace without feeling too overwhelmed.

Give Yourself Time

Without a doubt, setting priorities can be overwhelming. I encourage you to take a rest in between. Even God rested on the seventh day when He created the universe (Genesis 2:2). If you try and do everything all at once, you may feel burned out. Follow the Lord's example by taking a break in-between completing your priorities. When you're well rested, you can continue and feel at ease. You can also use this rest time to look over your list and update it if need be. If you forgot to cross some things off that you've completed, you can also spend some time updating it. You're not working on completing your priorities; instead, you're becoming more organized with your day while resting at the same time.

When Are You Most Productive?

Is it during the day or in the afternoon? In the morning? When the kids are in bed? Depending on when you are most productive, you can set your time accordingly. If it's right after breakfast when the kids are in school and you've had your morning coffee, you can use that time strategically to complete your top priorities. This will help minimize distractions, even if they're small, such as helping your kids with homework or making lunch. You'll not only get more done during your high productivity hours, but you will feel more accomplished knowing you were able to focus on the tasks at hand.

Hold Yourself Accountable

One effective way of holding yourself accountable is having an accountability partner. Choose people you trust with whom you can share your priorities with and who can help keep you on track with completing them. By sharing your priorities with them, you set up a verbal contract with yourself to get things done, no matter what.

Setting Achievable Goals

As mentioned above, it is important that you set realistic goals–goals that you can get on board with and feel achievable to accomplish in a realistic timeframe. Setting these types of goals, rather than goals that feel very overwhelming, will help you become more productive with your time, instead of feeling like procrastinating because you are way in over your head and think that your goals are impossible to accomplish.

If you're setting a goal that seems impossible to accomplish, there could be a few reasons why this is happening:

- **There is no heart connection.** What does this mean? Your goals don't hold as much value to you as you think they do. In your mind, you're setting the goal, but in your heart, you don't know why you're setting the goal in the first place. This makes a huge difference if you dream of your goals coming to fruition. Your goals must align with your heart because that way, you'll feel more inclined to accomplish them, regardless of the challenges that arise.

- **They are generic.** Generalizing your goals also makes a huge difference. When setting realistic goals, I encourage you to be as specific as possible. When writing down your goals, add as many details as you can. That way, you can become crystal clear about why you want to achieve them and what you desire the outcome to be.

- **You don't feel supported.** It's always better to accomplish things as a team. Two heads are always better than one. If you're trying to accomplish a goal, but there isn't anyone to hold you accountable or support you, you'll eventually get burned out and feel like it's a waste of time. By sharing your goals with others, as mentioned above, you will be more supported rather than trying to accomplish them on your own, which in turn, will motivate and encourage you to keep moving forward until you've reached your desired outcome.

Whose Money Is It, Anyway?

In The *Peaceful Haven,* Janelle Esker speaks of our relationship with money in this sense: "To have a healthy relationship with money, we must acknowledge this profound truth: God owns everything. Our money is His money" (2021).

When we think about this statement, it is also important to acknowledge that God provides us with abundance everywhere. He also provides us with the money we need to survive. In 1 Chronicles, it says this about money: "Yours, Lord, is the greatness and the power and the glory and the majesty and the splendor, for everything in heaven and earth, is yours. Wealth and honor come from you; you are the ruler of all things. In your hands are strength and power to exalt and give strength to all" (*NIV*, 2011/1973, 1 Chronicles 29:11-12).

To have a healthy relationship with money, we must understand what God wants us to do with it and obey His will. Knowing that our money is God's money, when we have a healthy relationship with money, we have a healthy relationship with God.

Below are a few ways that can help you strengthen your relationship with money.

Use God's Money to Do Fun Things

Matthew 6 says, "But seek first his kingdom and his righteousness, and all these things will be given to you." (*NIV*, 2011/1973, Matthew 6:33). It is important to have fun with the abundance God has given you, but it is also important to seek His word first. Ask Him what He wants you to do with this provision. What does He want you to experience? Perhaps He wants you to give to the poor or spend some time with your family on a vacation. By listening to God's will and being obedient, He will help you create a healthier relationship with money.

Strengthen Your Money Mindset

To have a healthy relationship with money, it is important you strengthen your money mindset. You cannot have a healthy relationship if you still feel like you're living in scarcity. Strengthening your money mindset means that you are shifting your money story to believing that you are already living in abundance, rather than believing you are in scarcity. Your money story could be that of scarcity, lack, and past financial mistakes. By letting go and reminding yourself that you are always growing, you can shift into believing you are abundant. This shift, although it appears small, can make a *huge* difference in your relationship with money.

Practice Gratitude

One of the highest values when it comes to abundance is gratitude. Feel grateful for all that you have, even if it is small. Express gratitude for the cappuccino you were able to purchase, the food in your fridge and pantry, paying the bills every month, the clients you have in your business, and the job that is helping you produce income—be grateful for it all. God gave you these provisions; be sure to thank Him for all that you have and all that He will give you.

Stop Comparing Yourself to Others

As humans, we are used to comparing ourselves to our friends, family, and neighbors. We may feel they have a better house or car than us. Maybe they go on more vacations, or their kids attend better schools. Having a healthy relationship with money means that what you currently have is what is meant for you. Just because you feel someone else has something better than you, it doesn't mean it's true. That's what the enemy wants us to believe. The devil wants to steer us away from God's love and provision, so he will do anything he can to throw us off course into thinking that God is not providing for us as much as He does for others. By stopping the comparison, a couple of things happen: 1) We release toxicity and negative comments from our lives that may cause us to think that we are not living an abundant life, and 2) We get back on track with gratitude and appreciation for the things that God does provide us with, which in turn helps us feel blessed knowing that He is always providing, regardless of our circumstances.

Strengthen Your Relationships

One surefire way of creating a harmonious balance in your life so you're not thinking all about money is to strengthen the relationships with your friends and family.

These people are the ones that God has blessed you with. Even if it's for a season, they are meant to be a part of your life, and you are meant to be a part of theirs. It is important you feel grateful for these relationships. Find ways to strengthen the bond you have with the people you love and care about the most. If you haven't spoken to your sister in a while, call her. Ask her to go out for coffee. See how she's doing. Show her you care. Develop a stronger bond with your kids by playing with them and taking time out of your busy day to spend time with them.

Here are a few tips that can help you strengthen your relationships:

- **Make time to spend together.** Create a space where you can do things together that you enjoy.

- **Learn more about who they are.** What do they like to do? What do they like or don't like? Get to know them inside and out.

- **Show that you care.** Listen to them and lend an ear or a hug, when needed.

- **Feel grateful for who they are.** That may mean that you don't agree with each other at times. That's okay. Appreciate their uniqueness.

- **Help them as much as you can.** Do what you can to serve them. If they're feeling stressed and overwhelmed, take them out for coffee and allow them to vent. If they're sick, bring them soup or offer to pick up their groceries.

Practice Self-Care

If you want balance in your life, taking care of yourself is important. It's that simple.

There are many ways that you can indulge in self-care habits that will help you pay attention to your needs. Here are a few:

- **Focus on your sleep hygiene.** Are you ensuring to get six to eight hours of sleep every day? If not, I encourage you to review your sleep hygiene. When you are well-rested, you become more productive during the day.

- **Engage in consistent exercise.** Be active throughout the day. Create a workout routine that you can do every single day. Exercising regularly gives you more energy and decreases fatigue.

- **Nourish your body.** Just as exercise is important, so is what you put into your body. Eat healthy food that gives you energy and vitality. Refrain from eating food that decreases your energy, such as pop, chips, or other junk food.

- **Stick to a self-care routine.** Create a routine that you can stay committed to, even when your friends and family try to steer you in a different direction. When it comes to committing to your self-care activities, it is okay to say no to your loved ones when they want to go out or eat food that is not right for their body. When you take care of yourself, you take care of your family at the same time.

- **Get out in nature.** Treating yourself to a brisk walk around the park or your neighborhood can bring automatic balance into your life. Spending time in nature can help give you the rest that you need to then focus on your priorities.

- **Invest in personal development.** Go to a self-care and wellness retreat, read a book on personal growth and development, and participate in classes such as yoga, mindset training, or Pilates. In doing so, you not only gain wisdom, as we explained in Chapter Six, but you also practice self-care by focusing on your body, mind, and spirit.

Living a Spiritual Life

There is no doubt that to create balance in our lives, we need to take the spiritual path. Genesis 1:27 reminds us that "God created man in his own image" (*NIV*, 2011/1973). When reflecting on this verse, we must understand that we must do all that we can to live as the Bible instructs us to live, while also –teaching others about how to live according to the gospel. By using the Bible as an example for our lives, we can become an example to others.

So, as believers, how can we live based on what the Bible says? Here are a few ways:

- **Live as God wants us to live.** Philippians 1:27 says, "Whatever happens, conduct yourselves in a manner worthy of the gospel of Christ. Then, whether I come and see you or only hear about you in my absence, I will know that you stand firm in the one Spirit, striving together as one for the faith of the gospel" (*NIV*, 2011/1973). In other words, shift our mindset and renew our spirit, release the negativity that holds us back, and act in righteousness, knowing that God's love is always with us.

- **Stand firm knowing that Christ's spirit is within us.** The Word in Philippians also says, "Stand firm in one spirit." No matter what, help and serve together. The more we grow to love and support one another, the more Christ's love grows within us, and the more we become unified as one community.

- **Our confidence in spirit grows, despite enemy attacks and other challenges.** The following verse in Philippians reminds us that "without being frightened in any way by those who oppose you. This is a sign to them that they will be destroyed, but that you will be saved—and that by God" (*NIV*, 2011/1973, Philippians 1:28). When we have no fear in the face of enemy attacks, our confidence in the spirit grows, knowing that God has already fought our battles for us. Overcoming fear and facing our challenges with confidence becomes our spiritual testimony that demonstrates Christ's love. Romans 8:37 says, "We are more than conquerors" (*NIV*, 2011/1973).

Help Those in Need

In John 15, God's word urges us to "love each other just as I have loved you" (*NIV*, 2011/1973, John 15:12). This verse teaches us how to help and serve others that come across our path. It teaches us about compassion and reverence toward others so that we may be kind and forthcoming.

As we are created in the likeness and image of God (Genesis 1:27), we are meant to help others as much as we can and make sacrifices just as Christ did when He died for our sins and for us to have freedom.

By helping others, we can benefit in the following ways:

- **Emotionally:** When we become invested in helping others, we not only feel good but our confidence and self-esteem grow at the same time. If we're shy, by learning to help others in need, we can become less socially anxious and get comfortable with hanging around people.

- **Physically:** By helping others, we can become more active. For example, if you help your elderly neighbor shovel their sidewalk from the evening's snowfall, you gain muscle strength as well as stamina and endurance. Not only are you becoming physically fit, but your neighbor is also grateful that you are helping them. By engaging in daily activity, you reduce stress and anxiety, and in turn, you are doing something good for those you care about.

Power of Prayer

To me, balance equals prayer. Praying offers incredible power that at times we neglect to take advantage of. 1 Chronicles says this about the power of prayer: "Look to the Lord and his strength; seek his face always" (*NIV*, 2011/1973, 1 Chronicles 16:11).

When we are struggling or facing a challenge, I find that praying and seeking guidance from the Lord helps tremendously. There is a sense of peace and joy that washes over me every time I pray and ask God for direction. When we pray, it is important to stay quiet and wait for the Lord to answer. God always has His perfect timing with His answers. One thing I learned is to allow my heart to stay open to receiving the answer to my prayer, as well as Christ's guidance. As a human and sometimes as a believer, this is a hard thing to do, especially when 1) We are praying about something we want the answers for now and 2) We have already decided the outcome. The trick is to be open to the unexpected, as already stated earlier in the chapter. If God says no, then it's no. If He says to wait, it is important to obey. There is a high spiritual reason we have been told to wait—it is important to trust it, no matter what it is, knowing that God never steers us wrong.

Benefits of Prayer

There are many benefits to praying and lifting your requests to the Lord that I'd like to share with you in hopes that they can empower you to pray often:

- It helps you to remain focused.

- It gives you the light of hope in the face of challenges.

- It helps you have a deeper connection with the Lord.

- It provides guidance when you're struggling.

- It can restore your peace.

- It can help heal.

- It can give you strength and confidence.

- It can help give you clarity.

- It can help restore kindness in your heart.

- It can help you forgive yourself and others.

- It can remind you that you're never alone.

Meditation

To help sum up this chapter, I'd like to recommend a few bible verses regarding balance and money that you can meditate on. As with the others in the previous chapters, I encourage you to reflect on the ones that resonate with you the most, as you seek God's guidance in helping you understand what the verse means for your life.

Bible Verses on Balance

- Ecclesiastes 3:1
- Isaiah 28:24
- Matthew 23:23
- Micah 6:8
- 2 Thessalonians 2:16
- Deuteronomy 15:10

Bible Verses on Money

- Deuteronomy 7:13
- Deuteronomy 8:18
- Deuteronomy 28:2
- Deuteronomy 28:6
- Deuteronomy 28:11-13
- Malachi 3:10-12
- 2 Peter 1:3-4
- Philippians 4:19
- Proverbs 10:22

- Proverbs 13:22
- Proverbs 22:4
- Proverbs 22:4
- Psalm 24:1
- Psalm 34:10
- Psalm 37:25
- Psalm 68:19
- Psalm 84:11
- Psalm 90:17
- Psalm 115:14
- Psalm 145:15

Now that we've concluded this chapter, I trust that it has helped you see how to create balance in your life. Every day, we have a choice to either create balance in our lives where we have peace, joy, and fulfillment, or we can continually experience stress and anxiety because we don't feel productive in anything we do.

Some of the highlights of this chapter include:

- Money is not everything. Of course, we need it to survive every day, but it is important to create a balance between money and everything else we do so that money doesn't become the only objective.

- It is important to establish priorities as much as possible. Setting priorities helps us become more organized in our daily life, and by crossing them off our list, we feel more productive.

- It is important to have a healthy relationship with money. Our money is God's money so what we do with money reflects our relationship with God.

- Prayer is powerful. The more we pray, the more peace we feel in our hearts.

- Taking care of ourselves should be our top priority. When we take care of ourselves, we can take care of others.

- We are created in the likeness and image of God (Genesis 1:27), and therefore, it is important to live a spiritual life by the gospel as much as we can.

The next and last chapter will summarize everything that we have been exploring in this book so you can truly learn to live an abundant and prosperous life.

Chapter 8:
All Roads Lead to You

Now that you know these things, you will be blessed if you do them. –John 13:17

In the last seven chapters, we have gone through so many tidbits of information. You have acquired so much wisdom and knowledge that you can now take with you. As we discussed in Chapter Six, knowledge is not power unless wisdom is involved, so I encourage you to take what you've learned within this book, meditate on the verses I've shared, and find ways to apply the knowledge to your life.

Take notes or write freely on anything and everything that you have learned. Think of this as an extra self-care moment where you're spending time with God, embracing His love, strengthening your relationship with Him, and appreciating all the abundance He has surrounded you with. This is your time to have a deeper relationship with your faith—I encourage you to embrace it for all its worth.

Healing Is Not Linear

My value is not at all tied to my experiences or my pain. It is solely tied to Jesus Christ; He says I'm worth dying for. –Laura Miles

When we're experiencing trauma or hardship, we wish it would all go away, and that we would heal quickly. However, as we discussed in Chapter Three, healing takes time, forgiveness (of ourselves and others), humility, and finally, faith in God's power to restore our spirit. We must stay on His path, no matter the obstacles we encounter, so we can come out on the other side bathed in light and filled with hope.

If you're currently in a difficult situation, I'd like to share with you a few bible verses that have helped me in my healing journey. Perhaps they can also help you by encouraging you to never give up, no matter how much darkness you're facing:

- Psalm 31:24

- 1 Corinthians 16:13

- Philippians 4:13

- 2 Chronicles 15:7

- Psalm 28:7

- Proverbs 3:5-6

- Isaiah 26:4

- Psalm 112:6-7

- Psalm 37:5

- Matthew 19:26

- Job 42:2

If you seek God in everything you do and, in every trial, you face, you will always get up, even if you stumble. Even if you don't have strength, He will be your strength, your guide, your compass. "This too shall pass" (*NIV*, 2011/1973, John 16:33).

Affirmations

Using affirmations is an amazing tool to help inspire, encourage, and strengthen your faith in times of trouble. You can create your own or find some on the internet that you relate to. I encourage you to say them regularly as they will aid in lifting your spirit.

Here are a few positive affirmations that you are welcome to use:

- Every single day, I grow in faith, hope, and love.

- My strength is being renewed every day.

- I love, trust, and have faith that my Lord will see this through.

- I have confidence in God that this too shall pass.

- I am safe and comforted in God's loving arms in every moment.

- I am living a beautiful and abundant life every day.

- In every moment, I feel abundant, knowing I am God's child.

- I feel safe and protected knowing God has already won my battles for me.

- Every day that passes, I feel more at peace than I did the day before.

- I am healed and fully restored in Jesus's name.

- I have unshakeable faith knowing that the Lord is always with me.

There you have them: the keys to living an abundant and prosperous life, full of God's grace and love. I encourage you to follow the steps I've offered here to create your own abundant life. Whenever you fall, He will show you how to get up strong and resilient. Put your faith in Him, and He will show you a magnificent life.

Conclusion

Live by faith, not by sight. –2 Corinthians 5:7

By reading this book from cover to cover, you have taken a *big* step toward not only achieving an abundant life but toward deepening your spiritual journey with the Lord. All the Lord asks of you is to live by faith, just as 2 Corinthians urges us to do. Live by faith, knowing that you are always provided for. Live by faith, knowing that you are never alone—God is always with you. Live by faith, knowing that you can choose to live an abundant life anytime you wish.

This book was meant to empower you into believing in yourself and have the confidence knowing your abundant life is only one choice away. God led you down my path and to reading this book because He heard your prayers. He knew you were perhaps struggling with your faith and perhaps you are currently going through challenges that you're unsure of how to overcome—the messages in this book are part of the light you are seeking.

To recap, here are some key takeaways from this book:

- **Chapter 1** invites you to consider how you see yourself and to change your thought patterns, so you remind yourself of how God sees you.

- **Chapter 2** shows you that living an abundant life is always a choice. You can refrain from scarcity, shift your story, and choose to acknowledge the abundance already in your life just like that!

- **Chapter 3** talks about the importance of humility and learning to let go of your pride and ego by focusing on being humble. It also reaffirms the power and value of forgiveness so you can live a life full of joy and peace.

- **Chapter 4** emphasizes the importance of freeing your mind by breaking away from the chains of negativity so you can embrace a positive mindset.

- **Chapter 5** discusses how to manage your emotions, so you are no longer controlled by negative emotions and instead seek to cultivate an abundance mindset.

- **Chapter 6** offers an exhilarating take on vision, encouraging you to embrace God's vision for your life and emphasizing the importance of wisdom, knowledge, and strategy.

- **Chapter 7** teaches you to be more productive when it comes to setting goals and priorities. We also discuss the importance of creating balance in our lives, where money is not the primary focus.

- **Chapter 8** ties everything together.

I can assure you that each section in the chapters has helped many women create their own testimonies. They allowed for a deeper relationship with God and enhanced their spiritual journey toward gospel living. They truly learned how to live an abundant life in the eyes of our Father in heaven.

Here's my last message for you: God always wants the best for you. He loves you unconditionally. You may have strayed from the path of faith, but that doesn't mean it's too late to get back on it. I encourage you to use the life lessons you learned here and carve a path toward a brighter and more fulfilling future. I know you can do it, and so does God! He believes in you wholeheartedly. Even though you may feel alone in this journey at times, I encourage you to remind yourself that God is with you. He will never leave you nor forsake you (Deuteronomy 31:8). His promise is right there in His word.

I also encourage you to share this book with other believers who are looking for spiritual guidance and wisdom from the Lord–those who have prayed for an abundant life, but who still feel like they are living in scarcity. This book is for them. The message in this book is what they need to hear so they can follow the path to righteousness once again.

Thank you for joining me on this journey. I wish you God's best as you continue down your spiritual path. If this has blessed you, I encourage you to write a testimony on Amazon—your testimony can help change someone's life. Thank you for being a vessel for them.

God bless you richly, abundantly, and fervently.

About Loretta (La-Rue') Duncan-Fowler

Loretta (La-Rue') Duncan-Fowler is a New York Times and Amazon Best Selling Author, Poet, Singer, Songwriter, Actress, and Spoken Word Artist.

La-Rue's love for writing started at the early age of 2 years old when she learned to write her ABCs and she hasn't stopped as a child she carried around a little wooden briefcase her uncle made her which included her poetry and journals. Her debut book, My Deepest Affections are Yours - Love Poems received wide recognition, however, it was La-Rue's Poetic Autobiography In Search of a Father's Love that received the coveted Pacific Book Review Purple Star Award and a 5-star review in the US Review of Books.

A starred review recognizes books of outstanding quality and is one of the most prestigious designations in the book industry.

The anthology Unbreakable Spirit Rising Above the Impossible Co-authored with best-selling author and transformational coach Lisa Nichols made her a New York Times and Amazon Best Selling Author.

La-Rue' is a member of The American Poets Society and holds a Bachelor's Degree in Computer and Information Sciences and received honor and recognition from The Stanford University Journal of Pan African Studies for her poems Color, Blind, Deaf, and Dumb (a dedication to the survivors of Hurricane Katrina), Unconditional, and Mother Sonia (a dedication to poet Sonia Sanchez).

By sharing her ministry gifts, she uses them to counter the effects of suicide, hopelessness, lack, and insufficiency found in people today, to assist people in understanding that nothing they have ever been through can separate them from God's love!

You can connect with La-Rue' on her website at:

www.lorettalarueduncanfowler.com

References

Abundant life. (n.d.). New Life International. https://www.waterfortheworld.org/abundant-life

Abraham, L. (2016, January 22a). *Weekly devotional: Fruit of the spirit–Gentleness.* Grand Canyon University. https://www.gcu.edu/blog/spiritual-life/weekly-devotional-fruit-spirit-gentleness

Abraham, L. (2016, January 29b). *Weekly devotional: Fruit of the spirit–Self-control.* Grand Canyon University. https://www.gcu.edu/blog/spiritual-life/weekly-devotional-fruit-spirit-self-control

Allen, J. (2022, August 1). *Five steps to renewing your mind.* Open the Bible. https://openthebible.org/article/five-steps-to-renewing-your-mind/

A quote by Lao Tzu. (n.d.). Goodreads. https://www.goodreads.com/quotes/8203490-watch-your-thoughts-they-become-your-words-watch-your-words

Ballard, R. (n.d.). *Keeping your life in balance.* The Church of Jesus Christ of Latter-Day Saints. https://www.churchofjesuschrist.org/study/new-era/2012/09/keeping-your-life-in-balance?lang=eng

Ballenger, M. (n.d). *4 things that will happen when God is giving you a vision for your future.* Apply God's Word. https://applygodsword.com/4-things-that-will-happen-when-god-is-giving-you-a-vision-for-your-future/

BetterHelp Editorial Team. (2022, November 23). *What is Wisdom? Inside its definition, synonyms, and meaning.* BetterHelp. https://www.betterhelp.com/advice/wisdom/wisdom-definition-synonyms-and-meaning/?utm_source=AdWords&utm_medium=Search_PPC_c&utm_term=PerformanceMax&utm_content=&network=x&placement=&target=&matchtype=&utm_campaign=17990185911&ad_type=responsive_pmax&adposition=&kwd_id=&gclid=CjwKCAiAl9efBhAkEiwA4TorijM0pa5kqopUfQ-uTD-WgVW9GPEOK2ftw22vOGhFcSojws-boQ48YRoCBs4QAvD_BwE

BetterHelp Editorial Team. (2023, February 22). *Self-forgiveness: It's important for you.* BetterHelp. https://www.betterhelp.com/advice/self-esteem/what-is-self-forgiveness-and-why-is-it-important-to-your-mental-health/

Bible Study Tools Staff. (2021a, February 19). *Bible verses about abundance.* Bible Study Tools. https://www.biblestudytools.com/topical-verses/bible-verses-about-abundance/

Bible Study Tools Staff. (2021b, February 19). *Bible verses about vision.* Bible Study Tools. https://www.biblestudytools.com/topical-verses/bible-verses-about-vision/#:~:text=Give%2520me%2520a%2520greater%2520vision,3%253A16%252D17).

Bible Study Tools Staff. (2021c, July 21). *I will never leave you nor forsake you.* Bible Study Tools. https://www.biblestudytools.com/topical-verses/i-will-never-leave-you-nor-forsake-you/

Bible Study Tools Staff. (2022a, February 10). *Prayer bible verses.* Bible Study Tools. https://www.biblestudytools.com/topical-verses/prayer-bible-verses/

Bible Study Tools Staff. (2022b, December 28). *God's promises are in the bible.* Bible Study Tools. https://www.biblestudytools.com/topical-verses/gods-promises-verses-in-the-bible/

Bible verses about money. (n.d). Charis Christian Center. https://www.charischristiancenter.com/bible-verses-about-money/?gclid=CjwKCAjw5P2aBhAlEiwAAdY7dNp4dL8Erap XotNF1pLRwegbHuVY0qjmwXSOwDnUKy3W6xurJh8BUh oCv2sQAvD_BwE

Bonaguro, A. (2015, April 17). *Why paper cuts are so painful (And how Krazy Glue can help)* https://www.menshealth.com/health/a19537789/why-are-paper-cuts-so-painful/

Brain Facts–Healthy Brains. (2015). Cleveland Clinic. https://healthybrains.org/brain-facts/

Bring to the light that which is in darkness–Ephesians 5:11-14. (2011, April 14). Marriage After God. https://marriageaftergod.com/devotional-bring-to-the-light-that-which-is-in-darkness/#:~:text=Parenting%20Prayer%20Challenge-,Bring%20To%20The%20Light%20That%20Which%20Is,%E 2%80%93%20Ephesians%205%3A11%2D14

Brown, G. (2016, October 7). *How to live worthy of the gospel.* Bible.org. https://bible.org/seriespage/5-how-live-worthy-gospel

Building meaningful relationships. (n.d). The Church of Jesus Christ of Latter-Day Saints.

https://www.churchofjesuschrist.org/study/ensign/2018/08/
building-meaningful-relationships?lang=eng

Cherry, K. (2022, July 22). *5 reasons emotions are important.* VeryWell Mind.
https://www.verywellmind.com/the-purpose-of-emotions-
2795181

Chery, F. (2023, February 15). *Bible verses about never giving up.* Bible
Reasons. https://biblereasons.com/never-giving-up/

Clarke, J. (2015, January 7). *15 scriptures about taking action.* A Divine
Encounter. https://adivineencounter.com/15-for-15/

Cowen, A. (2018, May 9). *How many different kinds of emotions are there?*
Frontiers for Young Minds.
https://kids.frontiersin.org/articles/10.3389/frym.2018.00015
#:~:text=The%2520patterns%2520of%2520emotion%2520tha
t,%252C%2520joy%252C%2520nostalgia%252C%2520relief%
252C

Crossway. (2020, May 19). *10 key bible verses on wisdom and discernment.*
Crossway. https://www.crossway.org/articles/10-key-bible-
verses-on-wisdom-and-discernment/

Davis, T. (2018, December 28). *Self-care: 12 ways to take better care of yourself.*
Psychology Today.
https://www.psychologytoday.com/us/blog/click-here-
happiness/201812/self-care-12-ways-take-better-care-yourself

Deibert, B. (2022, April 4). *What is humility? Bible meaning and importance
today.* Salem Web Network.
https://www.christianity.com/wiki/christian-terms/what-does-
humility-mean-in-the-bible-why-should-we-be-humble.html

8 simple ways to save money. (2022). Bank of America. https://bettermoneyhabits.bankofamerica.com/en/saving-budgeting/ways-to-save-money

Esker, J. (2021, September 22). *Bible verses to encourage a healthy relationship with money.* The Peaceful Haven. https://www.thepeacefulhaven.com/bible-verses-to-encourage-a-healthy-relationship-with-money/#:~:text=Both%20riches%20and%20honor%20come,to%20give%20strength%20to%20all.

Fernando, J. (2022, August 15). *What is financial literacy and why is it so important?* Investopedia. https://www.investopedia.com/terms/f/financial-literacy.asp

Ferrari, P. (2015, November 13). *Weekly devotional: Fruit of the Spirit - Kindness.* Grand Canyon University. https://www.gcu.edu/blog/spiritual-life/weekly-devotional-fruit-spirit-kindness

Ganti, A. (2023, February 4). *Net worth: What it is and how to calculate it.* Investopedia. https://www.investopedia.com/terms/n/networth.asp

Glasbergen, R. (2005). *The importance of helping others.* Glasbergen.com. https://www.washburn.edu/student-life/recreation-wellness/employee-wellness/documents/Helping-Others.pdf

Groenewald, A. (2019). *See yourself as God sees you: 3 thought patterns to correct.* The Life. https://thelife.com/see-yourself-as-god-sees-you

Hall, A J. (n.d). *The importance of prayer in our daily lives and how it can benefit us in many ways.* Think Eternity. https://thinke.org/blog/the-importance-of-prayer-in-our-daily-lives

Hare, D. (2020, August 20). *10 benefits of owning land.* APXN Property. https://apxnproperty.com/benefits-owning-land/

Helmig, L. (2017, December 6). *The Faith of a first lady: Eleanor Roosevelt's Spirituality.* Truman Library Institute. https://www.trumanlibraryinstitute.org/faith-first-lady-eleanor-roosevelts-spirituality/#:~:text=%E2%80%9COne's%20philosophy%20is%20not%20best,she%20is%20remembered%20as%20today

Hetrick, O. (2012, October 30). *The seven senses.* Joyful Star. https://missjoyh.wordpress.com/2012/10/30/the-seven-senses/

The importance of managing emotions. (n.d). Health Hub. https://www.healthhub.sg/programmes/186/MindSG/Caring-For-Ourselves/Managing-Our-Emotions-Adults#:~:text=At%2520times%252C%2520we%2520feel%2520overwhelmed,and%2520overcome%2520any%2520challenges%2520ahead.

Indeed Editorial Team. (2023, February 3). *How to set priorities in 4 steps (plus effective strategies).* Indeed. https://www.indeed.com/career-advice/career-development/how-to-set-priorities

Inspirational Quotes by Sandra Carey. (n.d). Right Attitudes. https://inspiration.rightattitudes.com/authors/sandra-carey/

Jackson, B. (2017, June 18). *Top 15 bible verses focused on God.* Everyday Servant. https://everydayservant.com/top-15-bible-verses-focused-god/

Keithley, Z. (2021, May 11). *40 positive affirmations for faith, hope, and trust.* Zanna Keithley. https://zannakeithley.com/40-positive-affirmations-for-faith-hope-and-trust/

King James Version. (1987). Bible Gateway Online. https://www.biblegateway.com (Original work published 1973)

King James Version (2021). King James Bible Online. https://www.kingjamesbibleonline.org/Hebrews-13-21/ (Original work published 1611)

Leading Effectively Staff. (2020, January 15). *How to set achievable goals (that align with your values).* Center for Creative Leadership. https://www.ccl.org/articles/leading-effectively-articles/achievable-personal-goals-align-with-values/

Lee, A. (2019, December 29). *7 scriptures on balance in our lives.* Words by Andy Lee. https://wordsbyandylee.com/7-scriptures-on-balance-in-our-lives/

Lindberg, S. (2021, April 8). *Can counseling help with depression?* Verywell Mind. https://www.verywellmind.com/depression-counseling-4769574

Living the gospel of Jesus Christ. (n.d.). The Church of Jesus Christ of Latter-Day Saints. https://www.churchofjesuschrist.org/study/manual/general-handbook/16-living-the-gospel?lang=eng

Maintain your good credit. (n.d.). Wells Fargo. https://www.wellsfargo.com/financial-education/credit-management/good-credit/

McCallum, D. (n.d.). *Vision and Christian leadership.* Dwell Community Church. https://dwellcc.org/learning/essays/vision-and-christian-leadership#:~:text=In%20the%20Bible%2C%20the%20word,(Numbers%2012%3A8).

McDaniel, D. (2023, February 16). *Is "This too shall pass" a bible verse? What God's word says about suffering.* iBelieve. https://www.ibelieve.com/faith/this-too-shall-pass-is-not-a-bible-verse-finding-hope-in-what-god-really-says-about-our-suffering.html

Mental health disorders and definitions. (n.d.). American Academy of Clinical Psychology. https://www.aacpsy.org/definitions

Merriam-Webster. (2023, February 6). Abundance. https://www.merriam-webster.com/dictionary/abundancehttps://www.merriam-webster.com/dictionary/abundance

Merriam-Webster. (2013). Humility. https://www.merriam-webster.com/dictionary/humility

Murphy, L. (n.d). *The non-linear journey to healing.* Christian Today. https://christiantoday.com.au/news/the-non-linear-journey-to-healing.html

New International Version. (2011). Bible Gateway Online. https://www.biblegateway.com (Original work published 1973)

Noyes, P. (2022, February 8). *What are the fruits of the spirit? Bible meaning and examples.* Christianity. https://www.christianity.com/wiki/holy-spirit/what-are-the-fruits-of-the-spirit.html

The Oracles. (2019, October 2). *Real estate is still the best investment you can make today, millionaires say—here's why.* CNBC Make It.

https://www.cnbc.com/2019/10/01/real-estate-is-still-the-best-investment-you-can-make-today-millionaires-say.html

Owens, N. (2017, March 6). *4 things everyone should know about humility*. Active Christianity. https://activechristianity.org/4-things-everyone-should-know-about-humility

Ross, S. (2022, March 22). *What is a good debt ratio (and what is a bad one)?* Investopedia. https://www.investopedia.com/ask/answers/021215/what-good-debt-ratio-and-what-bad-debt-ratio.asp

Ryan, J. (2019, October 2). *What does James 2:26 mean by 'Faith without works is dead?'.* Salem Web Network. https://www.christianity.com/wiki/bible/faith-without-works-is-dead-james-2-26-meaning.html

Sensory integration: Know the basics. (2019). Pathways.org .https://pathways.org/topics-of-development/sensory/

Shively, E. (2014, August 31). *Commentary on Romans 12: 9-21.* Working Preacher. https://www.workingpreacher.org/commentaries/revised-common-lectionary/ordinary-22/commentary-on-romans-129-21-5

Sommerfeldt, S. (2019, November 1). The healing power of journaling. Loving Roots. https://www.lovingrootsproject.com/allblogposts/the-healing-power-of-journaling

Sorren, M. & Berry, E. (2022, October 12). *31 bible verses about helping others in need without recognition.* Woman's Day.

https://www.womansday.com/life/inspirational-stories/g30539201/bible-verses-helping-others/

Stanley, B. (2020, April 27). *25 bible verses on forgiveness to bring you peace.* Compassion UK Christian Child Development. https://www.compassionuk.org/blogs/bible-verses-on-forgiveness/

Stories of calling. (n.d). The Church of England. https://www.churchofengland.org/life-events/vocations/stories-calling

Strondak, K. (2018, April 25). *Three ways God wants you to use your imagination.* Core Radiate. https://www.coreradiate.com/blog/imagination

Tams, L. (2016, December 12). *The importance of forgiveness.* Michigan State University. https://www.canr.msu.edu/news/the_importance_of_forgiveness

Taylor, K. (2019, December 30). *16 bible verses about God's calling for our lives.* World Vision Advocacy. https://worldvisionadvocacy.org/2019/12/30/16-bible-verses-about-gods-calling-for-our-lives/

10 ways to build a healthy relationship with money. (n.d.). Desert Financial Credit Union. https://www.desertfinancial.com/News-And-Knowledge/Build-Healthy-Relationship-With-Money

30 bible verses on emotions. (2021, March 15). Coffee With Starla. https://coffeewithstarla.com/bible-verse-on-controlling-emotions/

Vadlamani, S. (n.d.). *Abundance mindset: Why it's important and 8 ways to create it.* Happiness. https://www.happiness.com/magazine/science-psychology/abundance-mindset/

Walker, K. (2022, June 20). *What does it mean to wait on the Lord?* Salem Web Network. https://www.christianity.com/wiki/christian-terms/what-does-it-mean-to-wait-on-the-lord.html

Watermark Community Church. (2020, December 24). *Why can't I forgive myself?* https://www.watermark.org/blog/cant-forgive-myself

Westmoquette, M. (2013, November 21). *Why daily practice is important.* Everyday Mindfulness. https://www.everyday-mindfulness.org/why-dail-practice-is-important/

What are the different ranges of credit scores? (n.d.). Equifax. https://www.equifax.com/personal/education/credit/score/credit-score-ranges/

What does Ephesians 2:6 mean? (n.d.). Knowing Jesus. https://dailyverse.knowing-jesus.com/ephesians-2-6

Why study bible verses about wealth and prosperity? (n.d.). Solomon Success. https://solomonsuccess.com/how-to-become-wealthy/

Wolstenholm, J. (2019, December 27). *What does the bible say about vision?* Minno Kids. https://www.gominno.com/parents/what-does-the-bible-say-about-vision/

Wise Valdes, K. (2020, March 30). *The fruit of the holy spirit: What is love?* Osprey Observer. https://www.ospreyobserver.com/2020/03/the-fruit-of-the-holy-spirit-what-is-love/

Made in the USA
Las Vegas, NV
01 May 2024